# America Doesn't Owe You a Living

# America Doesn't Owe You a Living

## Success Is Your Choice

### ROBERT UNGER & JOHN KUPILLAS

Wynwood
A DIVISION OF
Baker Book House Co

Published by Wynwood Press
a division of Baker Book House Company
P.O. Box 6287, Grand Rapids, MI 49516-6287

Printed in the United States of America

**Library of Congress Cataloging-in-Publication Data**

Unger, Robert M.
    America doesn't owe you a living : success is your choice / Robert Unger and John Kupillas.
      p.   cm.
    ISBN 0-922066-91-4
    1. Success. 2. Success in business. 3. United States—Moral conditions. I. Kupillas, John H. II. Title.
BJ1611.2.U54   1994
158'1—dc20                            94-3715

The poem appearing on page 63 copyright © 1972 by SMI/USA, Inc. Used with permission.

The article on page 76 appeared in *New York Newsday* December 25, 1988. Used with permission of the publisher.

# Contents

# ACKNOWLEDGMENTS

We thank God for parents who gave us values (Rose and Alex Unger, and Mary and John Kupillas), and wives (Phyllis Unger and Marie Kupillas) who share those values so that we can raise children (Adam, David, and Samantha Unger, and Lauren, John, and Stephen Kupillas) with those same values. We also thank God for the values that gave birth to America.

*Dear Great, Great, Great Grandchild,*

We may not be around when you are old enough to read. Therefore, we pray that this book will serve as a useful guide to you as you travel through life. The advice it contains has been developed as a result of many years of contemplation and learning. The learning has often come the hard way—through mistakes and setbacks. If you adopt some of the ideas and attitudes that we suggest, maybe you can gain some wisdom and, at the same time, avoid some pain. As we say in the book, wise people learn from the experience of others, potentially wise people learn from their own experience, and fools just never learn.

We write this book at a time of great hope and great danger. While our American system continues to enhance the quality of life for the majority of its citizens, a growing number of people have become entrapped in the invisible cage of negative mental attitudes. This book was written also for them, to tell them that if they change their expectation of poverty into an expectation of abundance and their attitude of despair into an attitude of hope, anything is possible in this great country.

The answer to America's problems lies in getting back to the basics that built this country. Many of these basics are set forth in this book. You see, dear grandchild, this book promotes the philosophy of individual freedom and responsibility, a philosophy that has enabled Americans to have the highest standard of living on earth. It is also the philosophy that ensures success and fulfillment for the individual. On the other hand, a philosophy that denies individual responsibility and discipline precludes individual success and fulfillment. Once you realize that you are responsible for where you go in life, you will set goals and strive to attain them. The greatness of this country stems from the minds of great thinkers who realized that people could indeed exercise free will and act responsibly.

If you are to take responsibility for perpetuating the greatness of this country, you must first develop the greatness that is within you. You are the greatest you that ever was or ever will be.

When we were growing up, there was a lot of pressure for kids to fit in, to be part of the crowd. We were encouraged to fear being different. Please don't make that mistake. Be different.

Many people lead lives of quiet desperation; be different. Most people are doing what they don't like to do; be different. Most people are afraid of trying to get the things they dream about; keep trying, keep dreaming, and be different. A lot of kids are taking drugs because their friends are doing it and pushing them to join in; be different.

The people who succeed capitalize on their uniqueness. They find and develop that certain something that will set them apart from the pack. We were struggling lawyers in an overcrowded profession. As you'll find out in this book, becoming the "Singing Lawyers" made us different. We used our singing ability to establish ourselves as different from all other lawyers in attitude and style. We certainly were not afraid to attract attention.

After all, if you only want to be like everyone else, you're just going to be average. Average isn't very good at all. Why not be the best that you can be? No one can tell you how good that best can be. Why not give it a try and find out for yourself? You can never succeed if you don't try, and you can never fail unless you think you have failed. As long as you persevere and keep working toward your goal, you can't be counted out. Sooner or later, the person who wins is the person who keeps thinking, "I can do it," and keeps working at it.

Strike the word *can't* from your vocabulary. You may not know *how* to do something, but you certainly *can* do it if you take the time to learn *how* to do it.

The same is true for success. Anyone can be successful if he or she takes the time to learn how. We hope this book helps you learn how to get what you want out of life. However, that should be only the beginning. Continue reading books like this on the subject of achievement. Study other people who have lived lives of accomplishment. Your constant study will help you to keep growing inside as a person and growing outside in your relations with other people. It will also help you to teach your children and others.

Most of all, remember that you have greatness within you. Believe this absolutely. Seek out your greatness and you will surely find it. Maybe you can even write a book to pass on to *your* great, great, great grandchildren. Remember, success is out there. All you have to do is tune it in and realize that America doesn't owe you a living.

Love,
Bob Unger and John Kupillas

# INTRODUCTION

## *The Government Abuses a Minority Group: Achievers*

A chievers of the world unite! You have nothing to lose but your chains. We are writing in order to rally you around the defense of the American dream. After all, although you are only about 5 percent of America, you are responsible for the jobs and prosperity of the other 95 percent.

We (the authors) are two people who grew up in New York City and started our business with a negative net worth. Like scores of others before us, we believed that America was not a nation for the rich but a nation where those who had guts, determination, and drive could become rich. This is the reason this country has out-produced the rest of the world, while citizens of socialist nations stand in line to buy the basic essentials of life.

Unfortunately, it looks as if the president and the largely liberal Congress of the United States, along with their willing accomplices in the media, will not rest until all Americans are equal— equally poor.

13

The kind of achievement-bashing that has been conjured up by the Democrats and their media cohorts would make Karl Marx proud; it has been very effective in hoodwinking the American people through a disinformation campaign that even the KGB would envy.

As a result, we've been hit with a federal budget bill that will penalize productivity by placing higher income taxes on achievers and no reduction in the capital gains tax.

The achievement-bashers think the economy pie is unexpandable and therefore must be divided equally. They have apparently convinced many Americans that one can only become rich by making someone else poor. That's akin to saying one can only become fat by making someone else skinny.

Another commonly repeated lie is that the achievers pay no taxes. In fact, the achievers—1 percent of the American public—pay 27 percent of America's tax burden. Moreover, if the government were to confiscate 100 percent of the earnings of the so-called rich, it would fuel the federal government for only seventeen days. Guess who pays for the rest of the annual budget? That's right, the middle class.

Did you ever think about the fact that many Americans who earn between $100,000 and $200,000 a year have only 40 percent of their earnings left after the government steals their labor through income, real estate, Social Security, and excise taxes? And when they die, government shoots for the rest.

And it's precisely such individuals who will again take the tax hit, courtesy of the president and Congress through the latest budget bill.

Bill Clinton says the six-figure earners are rich, and therefore the wage earners feel no sympathy for the rich. But without the achievers, millions of wage earners would be on the unemployment line; without the entrepreneurs and other achievers, there wouldn't be any money to fund wage earners' unemployment insurance.

This great nation was not built on misdirected socialist policies that create equal economic deprivation for all. It was built on a capitalist system that encourages the quest for wealth enhancement; that system directly and indirectly benefits all those willing to join the quest.

The Democrats now bask in the joy of government discrimination against the achiever. Just turn on your television and you'll hear them saying, "We will make the rich pay for the wild party they had in the eighties under Ronald Reagan." Such statements reveal their ignorance: they think people get rich by having a party!

The politicians have been feeding at the public trough for so long they have forgotten what it means to really work to create wealth instead of confiscating it. Surely we can all remember friends or family members who worked two jobs and eighty-hour weeks to achieve success. They knew that motivation, hard work, and sacrifice—not partying—generate wealth.

# 1

# YOU ARE RESPONSIBLE FOR YOUR SUCCESS

*America Doesn't Owe You a Living*

Don't waste your time thinking of reasons for your failures and shortcomings. Instead, realize that the seeds of success were planted within you when you were born. You are responsible for bringing those seeds to fruition, not your mother, not your father, not society, and certainly not the government of the United States.

The seeds, and the power to grow them, are contained in the most awesome machine ever created: the human mind. No computer can come close to duplicating the goal-setting, goal-seeking, goal-attaining mechanism of the human mind.

## Success Is a Matter of Choice, Not Chance

We are listening to a local radio station. A lottery commercial blares away; a young man speaks inspirationally of his desire to move from his present position as mail clerk to become the president of the company.

Suddenly we hear laughter mocking the aspirations of the young mail clerk. The laughter is followed by the cynical rendition of "Fairy tales can come true, they can happen to you. . . ." This state-sponsored commercial for the New York State Lottery communicates a despicable message—that the dreams of this young man are nothing but a fairy tale. It tells us that the lottery is the way to gain success, that we should leave our future up to chance, and that setting high goals is laughable; all we need is "a dollar and a dream."

Well, a dream is not enough. Everyone dreams. What we need are goals. But few people set goals.

Goals are dreams with deadlines. Even a gambler knows that he must play the odds. Success depends on being a smart gambler, not a lottery player. The odds of gaining success by following the time-proven formulas for success are far greater than the likelihood of winning a million-dollar lottery. These formulas are the principles, attitudes, and actions that have been followed by great achievers throughout human history. If you follow these principles, success in life is a certainty. It is no longer a game of chance; it is a matter of choice.

## Freedom to Pursue Happiness

We who live in the United States of America should give thanks every day for this nation in which *anyone* who sets a *detailed and definite goal* can achieve that goal, regardless of the station of life into which he or she was born. America is a nation of *fluid* economic classes. The poorest individual at birth can obtain unlimited power, status, fortune, and fulfillment. Our founding fathers wrote this principle into our nation's birth certificate, declaring the pursuit of happiness to be an inalienable right, endowed by our Creator. As a result, true happiness and individual fulfillment can be attained in America, perhaps more than anywhere else on earth.

In America, our great traditions of hard work, determination, drive, and *individual* initiative have laid a solid foundation that can be built upon by any of us with the guts, drive, and determination to challenge ourselves to excellence. America is on *our* side, not his side, or her side, or their side, and any attempt to divide Americans by economic class should be dismissed as contrary to the principles of American free enterprise. Unfortunately, however, the class envy routine worked in the 1992 elections.

Bill Clinton realized that undisguised socialism doesn't go over big with the American people. So, with the cooperation of the media, he cleverly positioned himself in the public eye as a "new Democrat." He distanced himself from the "tax and spend" crowd; he promised a middle-class tax cut. The promise lasted up to election day. He began to speak of "investing" federal dollars, a new euphemism for government "spending." Guess what? Either way you can kiss your wallet goodbye.

Ironically, Bill Clinton's opponent, President Bush, was seen by many as more "liberal" than Clinton because he had broken his "read my lips—no new taxes" campaign pledge of 1988. Clinton struck a false populist note by pledging to remove the Republican "fat cats" from positions of power. Clinton was elected, of course, and wound up appointing a wealthier cabinet than the Bush and Reagan cabinets (most people are not aware that the Democratic Party garners more large donations than the Republican Party, yet the GOP is called the "party of the rich").

Thomas Edsall of the *Washington Post* stated that "crucial to his success has been Clinton's use of lan-

19

guage challenging the liberal orthodoxy even as he promotes a program that has the liberal wing of the Democratic Party in Congress as one of its strongest bases of support." In other words, Clinton used conservative code words in order to hoodwink the public into voting for socialism. Clinton had apparently learned from Dukakis and Mondale that if you let the voters know just how liberal you are, you will lose the election. In this regard, Clinton exhibited an ability to use one of the success techniques cited in this book: namely, learning from the mistakes of others. Unfortunately, the voters of America are about to get a lesson in learning from their own mistakes.

The Ten Commandments include "Thou shalt not covet." Socialism can thrive only when this commandment is disobeyed. Clinton was able to sell his campaign's "economic program" for "change" by appealing to the human tendency toward covetousness. As the Stanford University economist and scholar, Dr. Thomas Sowell, says, "The new anointed in Washington know that none of their ideas will fly under their true colors. Therefore they must set sail under false colors."

Such is the strategy behind all the demagoguery about how "the rich" are not paying their "fair share" (according to the politicians in Washington)—even though the top 10 percent of earners already pay 50 percent of all taxes. It seems that Clinton wants to give the impression that the rich were given their money by Ronald Reagan. And where did Ronald Reagan get the money? Well, of course, he emptied the pockets of the poor. Somehow when the money went from the poor man's pockets into the rich man's pockets, it multiplied in value. Only a man like Bill Clinton (who has spent his whole life feeding at the taxpayers' trough) could conclude that this is how one becomes wealthy. Those of his ilk would have everyone remain poor rather than

20

take the risk that someone might get rich. Clinton will only get away with this as long as he can fool the middle class into believing that it is worthwhile to be taxed to death as long as the same is done to the rich.

Ironically, the truth is that increasing income taxes on the wealthy never raises as much revenue as taxing the middle class. This is true for two reasons. First, there are vastly more people in the middle class than among the wealthy; therefore, that is where the money is. Second, most of the income among the wealthy is generated, not by wages, but by investment income. Therefore, when tax rates rise, the wealthy shift their investment capital away from companies and into tax-free investments. (During the 1992 campaign, for example, it was revealed that much of billionaire presidential candidate Ross Perot's money was invested in such tax-free investments.) Consequently, raising taxes on "the rich" becomes just another way of conning the middle class into allowing themselves to be soaked by our tax-hungry government. Because most middle-class people do not get their income from investment, they cannot avoid income taxes. Middle-class wage earners are pickpocketed through the withholding of their wages for taxes.

Furthermore, few Americans understand our free enterprise system enough to realize how withdrawal of investment brought on by excessive taxation also causes middle-class Americans to lose their jobs. An example of this is the "luxury tax" on jewelry, yachts, and automobiles over thirty thousand dollars. When this "covet thy neighbor" tax was instituted, middle-class America failed to realize that it would be them, not the wealthy, who would be hurt. The wealthy (who do not become wealthy because they are complete fools) simply cut back on luxury items or bought them overseas. The government suffered a net loss in tax revenues because all the carpenters, electricians, plumbers, and other middle-class workers deprived of their jobs by the luxury tax were no longer taxpayers themselves; they were in line collecting unemployment.

In New York, the home of Bill Clinton's tax-and-spend soul mate, Governor Mario Cuomo, the tax on hotel rooms has cost the hotel industry and the state tax coffers dearly, as hotel occupancy rates have declined. Undeterred by these examples, Clinton has taken to limiting business meal deductions. Watch out for all the restaurants that go out of business and all the restaurant workers that go on unemployment. As the song goes, "when will they ever learn?" Our advice: don't hold your breath.

Clintonomics is really a form of analysis that is often referred to as static economic analysis. In other words, it is economic analysis done solely on the basis of cold numbers without taking human nature and behavior into account. This is the type of analysis Karl Marx engaged in, as revealed by his formula, "from each according to his ability and to each according to his needs" (come to think of it, this sounds like the theme of today's Democratic Party). It apparently never dawned on Marx that the "from eaches" might begin to resent the "to eaches" who would be perceived as a bunch of "leeches."

Incredibly, in the Clinton lexicon, those who have achieved on the basis of their talent and hard work are viewed as greedy. Somehow congressional pay raises of 40 percent, passed in the dark of night, are not viewed as greedy in Washington, D.C. We certainly never hear about the need for them to "sacrifice and invest" in America. Far from sacrificing their own money, Congress throws taxpayer funds after outrageous pork barrel spending programs like the following:

$49 million for a rock and roll museum

$15 million to Dartmouth College as part of a jobs-creation program (a total of thirty-nine jobs were created, at a cost of $324,685 each)

$1.36 million for preliminary work on an $18.6 million project to turn Miami Boulevard into an "exotic garden for people"

$566 million (rising to $900 million later in 1991) to send American cows to Europe to participate in an "Export Enhancement Program"

$500,000 to study the effects of cigarette smoking on dogs

$107,000 to study the mating habits of Japanese quail

$19 million to study whether belching by cows and other livestock harms the ozone

$84,000 to study why people fall in love

$50,000 to prove that sheepdogs do, in fact, protect sheep

$46,000 to determine how long it takes to cook breakfast eggs

$90,000 to study the social and behavioral aspects of vegetarianism

$219,592 to teach college students how to watch television

$2,500 to investigate the causes of rudeness, lying, and cheating on tennis courts

$25,000 to find the best location for a new gym for the House of Representatives

$2 million to renovate one of the House restaurants

$350,000 to renovate the House beauty parlor

$6 million to upgrade the Senate subway system

(Sources: Citizens Against Government Waste, the Heritage Foundation, and the National Taxpayers Union)

Bill Clinton has convinced Americans that he can help them by raising their taxes in order to create public works jobs—and pay them with their own money. Economics writer Donald Lambro addressed the Clinton "stimulus" package of 1993:

> Clinton insists that spending, called an "emergency" appropriations bill, is needed to pump up the economy and create jobs. In fact, it is nothing but a bulging barrel of pork that will produce few if any real jobs. A few basic facts on what's in it:
>
> $2.54 billion in Community Development Block Grants, the notoriously wasteful Department of Housing and Urban Development program that has dished out billions of dollars for low priority projects to wealthy and comfortable middle-class communities under the guise of helping the poor.
>
> $23 million for the Environmental Protection Agency to give environmental grants to *Fortune* 500 corporations.
>
> $148 million to expand the Internal Revenue Service's computer system.
>
> $28 million for the District of Columbia to help pay its growing debts.

This is reinventing government?

White House Budget Director Leon Panetta said this new spending would create 219,000 jobs over the next year, though many jobs would not be created for several years. At least $4.4 billion of the package will not be spent until after October of 1994 and beyond because of the long-range nature of some of the public works projects, such as the EPA wastewater treatment grants.

Worse, the new employment that Clinton's spending stimulus plan would allegedly create would cost taxpayers an average of $89,013 per job. Compare that to the 365,000 jobs the private sector created in the month of February 1993 alone, without any spending stimulus—nearly 146,000 more in a single month than the Clinton plan would create in more than a year.

Moreover, the $16.3 billion that Clinton would use to finance these jobs must be taken out of the economy, through increased borrowing and taxation, potentially killing as many jobs as he creates.

There is a better and cheaper way to create real jobs and long-term economic growth: junk this ridiculous and wasteful stimulus package and exchange it for lower business tax rates—then get the government out of the way and watch the economy grow.

Another fiction that has pulled the wool over the eyes of America is the concept of taxing businesses. Get this straight: a business never pays taxes. Only customers pay taxes, in the form of higher prices charged by the business in order to absorb the tax amount. Furthermore, as taxes rise, businesses invest less in research and development. Where will our future scientific, medical, or industrial breakthroughs come from—the White House? Apparently the Clinton Administration thinks so; they believe that the State can make wiser investment decisions than successful business entrepreneurs (come to think of it, that's exactly what Lenin and Stalin thought).

Donald Lambro quotes the CEO of Cypress Corporation and other major corporate executives from Silicon Valley:

> "Essentially, the administration is arguing that by taking the money in the form of higher taxes and 'investing' it in subsidies, it can make better investments—create more jobs and wealth—than the venture-capital firms with which I invest—firms that are the envy of Japan and Europe," Rodgers says.
>
> "That logic defies common sense," he says. "Does anyone believe that Washington invests more effectively in high technology than the free market?"

25

The economic policy that is most needed now is the exact opposite of what Clinton is proposing. "Washington cannot create more companies like Silicon Graphics," Rodgers says. "The way to create more Silicon Graphics is to allow knowledgeable investors, steering their money through world-class venture capitalists, to try to fund just the right companies with just the right technologies at just the right time."

"Even these venture capital investment experts are wrong more often than they are right," he adds. "But surely they are right more often than Washington."

Don Valentine, founding venture capitalist and director of Apple Computer:

"To Washington I say, please do not help us. The world of technology is complex, fast changing, unstructured, and thrives best when individuals are left alone to be different, creative, and disobedient. Go help the Russians. Go help all the people who know how 'pork' works, and who want to be taken care of. But please do not help us: Anyone who thinks (raising) corporate taxes promotes employment does not understand the problem."

John Adler, CEO, Adaptec, a $300 million supplier of computer components and software:

"I am now deeply concerned about the trend of moving away from significant deficit reduction to significant increases in government spending. I am not in favor of increased government—even if it is directed to high technology."

L. J. Sevin, chairman of Cyrix, a computer chip supplier:

"The companies that the administration claims got a 'free ride' (in the 1980s) generated all the jobs and foreign exchange. And the so-called free ride probably earned the government a factor-of-ten return on the investment. Somehow, the administration's attitude seems to be that any money the government does not take in taxes is a gift to corporations."

Pierre Lamond, founder of National Semiconductor, a $1.6 billion computer chip company:
"Every dollar that is taxed away from individual investment or corporate R&D will weaken America's high technology companies."

Gil Amelio, CEO of National Semiconductor:
"Today, the top 5 percent of all wage earners pay 44 percent of all income tax—and if Clinton has his way this will increase further because he has campaigned on the basis of 'the politics of envy.' He wants to punish with high taxes Americans who have been successful— that is, the people we need to revitalize our economy."

Another bubble that needs to be burst is all this nonsense you hear about how wonderful a planned economy has worked in Europe and Japan. Pointing to foreign countries as examples is always an effective con since most Americans know little about what is really going on across the ocean. Therefore, a politician can make bogus claims about some European utopia, for example, and get away with it. The truth is, however, that unemployment rates are many times higher in Europe than they were in the 1960s. Japan is now in a terrible recession partly resulting from its government deciding what industries to invest in and, in all too many cases, making the wrong decision. While the U.S. constantly generates new start-up businesses, starting from scratch in Europe or Japan is exponentially more difficult. The rags-to-riches story is a uniquely American saga. Ironically, while the prime minister of Japan suggests new Reagan-like tax cuts, Bill Clinton is getting ready to take us from riches to rags.
As economist Paul Craig Roberts states:

27

The $1.5 trillion budget of the federal government is more than Great Britain or Italy—the fifth and sixth largest industrial countries—can produce. It would take almost a 100 percent tax on the GNP (Gross National Product) of Germany or France—the third and fourth largest economies in the world—to finance the U.S. government's budget. No one can seriously believe that U.S. citizens receive government services that are equal in value to the combined GNP of Canada and Latin America.

And Clinton wants us to tighten our belts so that he and Hillary can spend another $109 billion—more than the national income of Argentina—on their pet schemes.

How much room is in your budget to accommodate the new tax that Clinton wants to put on all forms of energy?

You are going to be taxed on the energy that you use to heat, cool, ventilate and light your home, cook your meals, run your refrigerator, and drive your car. You will pay the same tax again in the form of higher prices for the products and groceries that you buy, all of which are produced with energy.

Finally, let's set the record straight once and for all about Ronald Reagan. It seems that the liberals can't stand the fact that Ronald Reagan was one of the most effective and popular presidents of all time. Since Reagan has left office a nonstop barrage of public brainwashing by the media has caused the public to look at the Reagan presidency in a more negative light. Pay attention as seven liberal myths about Reagan are shattered before your very eyes courtesy of the *American Sentinel,* April 18, 1991.

Liberal Myth #1: The rich got richer, the poor got poorer. Truth: Between 1983 and 1989, real family income for the poorest 20 percent of Americans rose by 11.8 percent—a rate higher than for the majority of wage earners—and roughly equal to the 12.2 percent rise experienced by the richest 20 percent of the population. (Only four years prior to Reagan tax cuts, the real family income of the poor declined by 17.4 percent). Under Ronald Reagan, the overall number of persons living in poverty declined significantly, and by 1989 stood at its lowest recorded level.

Liberal Myth #2: The rich received tax cuts at the expense of the poor. Truth: Teddy Kennedy and other apostles of the welfare state say that Reagan's tax reductions were financed by slashes in social spending. Yet rapid GNP growth fueled by middle-class tax cuts financed a system of government transfers and taxes in the 1980s that significantly benefited the poor. When all government assistance programs are taken into account, including cash and non-tax benefits, the average income of households in the lowest 20 percent earning bracket was actually increased by $5,500 in 1989.

Liberal Myth #3: New Jobs created by Reagan policies were dead-end positions. Truth: Over twenty million jobs were created during the eighty-five-month economic expansion ushered in by Reaganomics. Eighty-two percent of the employment increase occurred in higher paying positions. Only 12 percent of the increase in employment occurred in the lowest-paid, lowest-skilled service occupations. Under Jimmy Carter, unemployment peaked at more than 10 percent by 1979. Reagan's policies, by contrast, caused unemployment to decline to a record sixteen-year low of 5.3 percent by 1989.

Liberal Myth #4: Black workers were left out in the cold by Reaganomics. Truth: Within the white-collar, high-paying managerial and professional occupations between 1983 and 1989, black employment rose by a stunning 30.4 percent. During that same period many low-income earners became middle-income earners and many middle-income earners became high-income earners.

Liberal Myth #5: Reagan's tax cuts for the rich caused a decline in the middle class. Truth: It is true that the middle class declined because of Reaganomics, from 57.8 percent to 52.9 percent. That is because many of them moved above the $50,000 threshold and into the high-income group. In fact, the number of families classified as low-income declined from 20.7 percent to 18 percent. The share of high-income families (over $50,000) increased sharply from 21.2 percent to 29 percent by 1989.

Liberal Myth #6: Reagan's tax cuts gave a "free ride" to high-income earners. Truth: Washington is so high-handed that it considers the policy of taxpayers keeping more of their hard-earned money to be a subsidy. Improved economic incentives established by Reagan caused taxpayers with taxable incomes of $200,000 or more to contribute $10 billion more to the treasury than if there had been no tax cuts at all.

Liberal Myth #7: Reagan's tax cuts hurt U.S. competitiveness. Truth: In a major departure from the dismal 1970s, Reaganomics sparked an impressive jump in manufacturing productivity. From 1981 to 1989, productivity growth averaged 3.7 percent each year, one-third faster than over the first post-war decades through 1973, and more than twice as fast as over the period from 1973 to 1981.

On the op-ed pages of the *New York Times* on February 18, 1993, Ronald Reagan defended himself in a piece aptly entitled, "There They Go Again":

> "First, we're going to raise the taxes on the people that did well in the 1980s," the Clinton Administration says. Did I hear that right? I'm afraid so! Do they really believe that those who have worked hard and been successful should somehow be punished for it? Is success in the 1980s, or any time for that matter, supposed to be something we as Americans are to be embarrassed about?
>
> I hate to confuse their economic thinking with a few facts, but if they were to look at the 1980s, they would find that America experienced its longest period of peacetime economic expansion in our history. They would find that America led the world out of a global

economic recession and that our economy was the envy of virtually every other nation. They would see that we created nearly nineteen million new jobs for Americans of all income levels. And it may shock the Clinton Administration to discover that most of the economic gains of the 1980s were made by low- and middle-income citizens, not the wealthiest Americans.

Earlier this week, President Clinton said, "I know we have learned the hard lessons of the 1980s." I didn't realize they were so hard to learn. The fundamental lesson to the 1980s was that when you cut taxes for everyone, people have the incentive to work harder and invest to make a better life for themselves and their families.

Somehow, as the Administration raises everyone's taxes, it wants us to take comfort in knowing that others are getting theirs raised even more. Unfortunately, that kind of "comfort" doesn't put food on the table of the hard-working middle class, buy new shoes for the kids or make it easier to pay the mortgage, let alone put some money aside for savings. The fact is, every dollar the politicians take back to Washington means less spending power for average Americans and more opportunity for the Federal bureaucracy to waste money.

No one can dispute that the enormous budget deficit is a major threat to the economic security of our country. But let us remember that deficits are caused by spending. By the very terms of our Constitution, only Congress has the power to spend.

For more than four decades, one party, the Democratic Party, has controlled the House of Representatives. The solution to the deficit problem is not to ask heavily taxed working Americans to "sacrifice" even more.

It's the big-spending liberals controlling the Congress who need to show some restraint and "sacrifice" a few of the pork-barrel measures they've been slipping past the taxpayers for far too long. Only when the Clinton Administration and Congress summon the will to put the brakes on Federal spending will they get the deficit under control.

31

The Reagan tax cuts of the 1980s are used by Clinton as an excuse to raise our taxes. Clinton claims that the greedy "tax cuts for the rich" are responsible for today's deficit. This is an unadulterated lie. As a result of the Reagan tax cuts, the amount of tax revenues actually doubled during the 1980s.

When taxes are cut, there is more money for the private sector to expand and invest; therefore, income and profits increase. A 30 percent tax on $100,000 of income still raises more tax revenues than a 50 percent tax on $50,000 of income; cutting taxes actually increases the amount of taxes collected by the government because it stimulates earnings and investments. This is precisely what happened in the 1980s as more taxes were generated from the nineteen million people put to work in new jobs. These jobs were created by those "greedy" Reagan tax cuts. However, for every dollar of tax revenues gained in the 1980s, the pork-crazed Congress spent approximately $1.75; that is why we have a budget deficit. America's problem is not that government taxes too little; America's problem is that government spends too much. This spending is the lifeblood and modus operandi of the career politician who operates just like a drug pusher operates. The drug pusher increases his customers by providing free drugs until his customers are hooked and therefore forced to pay him for the drugs. Likewise, the career politician hooks the voters on free programs. The voters then continue to elect the politician in order to continue to get their government fix.

In America today, taxes consume 40 percent of our gross national product. In just forty-five years, the average family has gone from paying 2 percent of its income in taxes to paying 24 percent of its income in taxes. In many parts of the country, federal, state, and local taxes combine to take 60 percent of one's income. As a result,

32

more and more latchkey children are generated due to the necessity for both parents to work. This in turn leads to increasing social problems (which gives the liberals another excuse to raise your taxes in order to solve the problems they created in the first place). This is a racket even the Mafia would envy.

It is time to put the brakes on the immoral confiscation of our hard-earned money. However, this will not occur unless we put the brakes on the confiscation of our Judeo-Christian moral foundation. Those who live under the laws of the Giver of the Ten Commandments must reject the "covet thy neighbor" rhetoric and policies of Washington. Economic prosperity can only exist hand-in-hand with moral prosperity.

> You cannot bring about prosperity by discouraging thrift.
> You cannot strengthen the weak by weakening the strong.
> You cannot help small men up by tearing big men down.
> You cannot help the poor by destroying the rich.
> You cannot lift the wage earner up by pulling the wage payer down.
> You cannot keep out of trouble by spending more than your income.
> You cannot further the brotherhood of man by inciting class hatred.
> You cannot establish sound social security on borrowed money.
> You cannot build character and courage by taking away a man's initiative and independence.
> You cannot help men permanently by doing for them what they could do for themselves.

This nation is not a configuration of the permanently rich, middle class, and poor. In point of fact, a new mil-

33

lionaire is made every sixty minutes in North America, and as long as we stick to the values that have made us great, such possibilities remain open. As Ronald Reagan loves to say, "America is not a nation of the rich, but a nation where everyone has the opportunity to get rich."

Remember, America doesn't guarantee equal results or happiness, only the pursuit of happiness. We alone are responsible for how we pursue happiness, success, and fulfillment in our lives.

## Education Fallacy

When we went through the ranks of the public school system in New York City, a number of negative-thinking professors tried to convince us that the Horatio Alger stories of rags to riches were a thing of the past. Not so; the Horatio Alger story can be repeated more easily today than ever before. Companies such as Nightingale-Conant Corporation in Lehigh, Illinois, and Success Motivation Institute in Waco, Texas, and scores of others produce educational tapes that will plant those seeds of success in your mind. *You* must water those seeds by constantly taking advantage of these wonderful tape programs that didn't exist in the days of the Carnegies and Rockefellers.

Modern technology has afforded us more leisure time than ever before. What is important is how this leisure time is used. If people chose to spend as much time planning their lives as they do planning their vacations, they would be able to afford more expensive vacations. Unfortunately, most people never plan their lives, and that is why 80 percent of all retirees, many having worked most of their life, are entirely dependent upon Social Security or whatever pensions they may have.

*You* are responsible for planning your life. *Only you* are responsible for listening to tape programs, reading books, and constantly working at and thinking about improving yourself. *Only you* are responsible for constantly writing out your goals and writing out your plans for attaining those goals.

It is amazing that so few of our nation's schools teach children to succeed. Today we have the ability to study, emulate, and model the habits and values of countless inspiring men and women who epitomize the greatness of our republic; yet our schools fail to do this. Isn't it just plain common sense to know that if one wishes to succeed, he or she should watch and emulate successful people (or watch to see what unsuccessful people do and then avoid doing it)?

One man with this kind of common sense and vision is actor Hugh O'Brian. Most readers will remember him for his starring role in the hit television series, *Wyatt Earp.* We believe, however, that Hugh O'Brian's greatest contribution to America is his establishment of HOBY (Hugh O'Brian Youth Leadership Foundation). The HOBY Leadership Seminars are held throughout the United States and abroad. They give young people an opportunity to interact face-to-face with distinguished leaders in business, industry, education, science, and government. These seminars help young people appreciate the greatness of our American system and the greatness within each of them. We were privileged to be guest speakers at the 1990 New York Leadership Seminar.

The theme of HOBY, like the theme of this chapter, is summed up in this excerpt from Hugh O'Brian's credo: "I believe every person is created as the steward of his or her own destiny with great powers for a specific purpose: to share with others, through service, a reverence for life in a spirit of love."

35

One of the most fallacious slogans of the modern era is "Knowledge is power." As a matter of fact, knowledge in a vacuum is of little value unless you are playing Trivial Pursuit. Knowledge in and of itself is of no consequence unless it is directed in the pursuit of a definite goal and a detailed plan for the attainment of that goal. In the words of former president Calvin Coolidge, "Nothing in the world can take the place of persistence. Talent will not; nothing is more common than unsuccessful men with talent. Genius will not; unrewarded genius is almost a proverb. *Education will not; the world is full of educated derelicts* [emphasis added]. Persistence and determination alone are omnipotent." A large percentage of all self-made millionaires never attended college. A large percentage never graduated from high school. It has been our experience that half of the educated people are employed by half of the high school dropouts in this country. Education without attitude is like a car without gasoline.

## Attainment, Not Entitlement

In the 1960s, America headed into a decline based on a bankrupt philosophy. The so-called "social scientists" who (in the words of popular New York radio talk show host Barry Farber) "are educated beyond their intelligence," began to tell us that a vicious criminal who had attacked an innocent victim was not to blame. It was the fault of society, poverty, homelessness, the government, and whatever other alibi could be thought up by pseudo-intellectuals looking out from ivory towers.

This distorted way of thinking rolled out the red carpet for an onslaught of violent street crime never before witnessed in this country. It led to the suffering of thousands of innocent victims and their families.

36

These same social scientists, arguing that poor people were incapable of achievement, embarked upon an orgy of wild spending for entitlement programs. While possibly well-intentioned, these programs have totally enslaved poor people and their families, sentencing them to a life without hope of freedom. In the name of some cockeyed quest for equality they have discouraged high standards so that everyone will be equally incompetent. If these people prevail, we are headed for a society that offers *equal* economic deprivation for all. The land of *attainment* will become the unproductive land of *entitlement.*

This notion that the individual is not responsible for his condition was extended to every problem encountered by individuals in this society. The government was blamed for the individual's poverty, and ironically, government was also seen as the solution for this same condition. The fact is that where you are now, and where you are going, are up to *you* and no one else. God has given us all the *free will* to decide what we *choose* to think and what we *choose* to do in relation to our thoughts.

We recently heard one of the highest elected officials in this nation address the graduating class of a famous university. He made the absurd assertion that people are wealthy because they have been blessed by God and that those who are poor are in that state because God has chosen not to bless them.

This brings to mind the ancient story of the real estate entrepreneur in the year 3000 B.C. who buys a rocky piece of worthless land. The seller thinks he has pulled a fast one, and all the D.T.s (Doubting Thomases) make a mockery of the gutsy entrepreneur. However, thanks to determination and persistence (or maybe benign ignorance), he works that land day in and day out. Eventually his work bears fruit, and the

37

pile of rock and sand is transformed into a flourishing garden. All the D.T.s come out of the woodwork to gaze upon this wondrous sight, and its fame spreads far and wide. One day a holy man comes down from the temple to view the garden. In a state of sheer amazement, he says, "This is truly a miracle, but you owe it all to God." The property owner thinks about the holy man's statement and thoughtfully responds, "You are right, God gave me the sun and the rain and life, but you should have seen this land when he had it all to himself." Get the message? *You* are responsible. It's been said before: God helps those who help themselves.

## Homelessness and Responsibility

Perhaps the most fashionable social cause today is homelessness. We can tell you from personal experience that since homelessness became the chic charity of the pseudointellectual elite and the defrauded well-intentioned, it has become increasingly difficult for many worthy causes to raise money. Playing It Safe, an organization in Syosset, New York, that is fighting to prevent an epidemic of kidnapping and abuse of children, struggles to get its fair share of funding. The Pride of Judea outpatient mental health facility struggles to survive. Obviously, there are unfortunate children and adults who become homeless due to fire, flood, or economic calamity. Many others, however, are homeless by choice—because of an addiction, for example, or an unwillingness to take responsibility for their own lives. Throwing money at this problem will not help. Many of the homeless are mentally ill people whom the so-called civil libertarians have liberated to sleep on sidewalk grates. A classic case in point occurred recently in New York City in the Billie Boggs case. The mayor at that time, Ed Koch, attempted to take homeless people off the streets in order to provide them with shelter and medical care. The ACLU sued the city of New York to force the city to release Billie Boggs from a medical institution and, effectively, to send her back to sleep on the sidewalk grate. Thereafter, the newspapers reported her arrest on drug charges. Next, Mayor Koch attempted to help large numbers of homeless people sleeping in the park next to city hall. He went to the trouble of bringing in vocational counselors who provided the homeless with jobs. Most of them didn't even bother to report to work. So who is to blame in cases like these? Who is to blame for the large numbers of homeless who are substance abusers?

At the same time that all too many able-bodied men and women *choose* not to work, Fox's Pizza has equipped itself to hire handicapped people, who are thrilled at having the opportunity for gainful employment. And scores of companies are advertising for elderly people to fill thousands of service positions because they cannot find enough people in younger age groups to work!

At the Human Resources Center in Albertson, New York, which offers rehabilitation and training for the handicapped, the Singing Lawyers had the honor and privilege of conducting a motivational talk. We were inspired to observe the determination, grit, and optimism of these courageous young people and their families. The audience there consisted of some of the least handicapped people we have ever seen. They have *chosen* to be ready, willing, and able to take on whatever challenges are presented to them for meaningful employment. They are resolved to utilize their special talents. They are "winners" who will undoubtedly leave a very positive mark on society.

## To Your Health

All of us are also responsible for the lifestyle we choose, a choice that affects the state of our health. We must accept responsibility for choosing a healthy lifestyle, instead of blaming God, fate, or genes.

The number one cause of death in this country is cardiovascular disease. This is essentially a disease of lifestyle based on following certain dietary patterns and patterns of exercise (or no exercise). Most fatal diseases are caused by our *choosing* to eat improperly, our *choosing* not to exercise, our *choosing* to think negatively, thereby arousing negative emotions. Fatalities are generally not caused by germs or viruses, but by an accumulation of poisons that we voluntarily consume: cholesterol, fat, cigarettes, drugs, alcohol, and so on. Nathan Pritikin was one of the brave pioneers in educating the general public to this fact. Our skyrocketing health-care costs could be greatly reduced if people would simply *choose* a lifestyle that promotes health instead of disease. Proper diet and exercise, combined with a positive mental attitude, are more effective and cost-efficient than any government-sponsored health insurance or socialized medicine program.

Dr. Howard R. Pyfer and his Wellness Center in Bellevue, Washington, illustrate the wisdom of the saying, "An ounce of prevention is worth a pound of cure." After twenty-two years of "sick people" medicine, he decided to devote his efforts to helping people stay well. "Take care of yourself in such a way that it will allow you to reach your goal," he said. "You have a choice." In other words, you are responsible for your health.

Modern medicine has also begun to recognize the importance of positive emotions in the healing of patients. *Emotions are the result of what we choose to think, and we are responsible for what we choose to think.* Negative emotions are not caused by external factors; they are caused by our reactions to external stimuli. Once we accept responsibility for our feelings, we will no longer blame external forces. In fact, even the negative emotion of worry or anxiety is caused by indecision. Once you think and act decisively, the worry seems to vanish. Negative emotions not only hinder the healing process but are often the root cause of the disease in the first place.

As attorneys, we have handled many personal injury cases. We have frequently witnessed severely injured people with positive mental attitudes who make seemingly miraculous recoveries. On the other hand, we have seen people whose lives lack purpose, meaning, and fulfillment become physically and mentally destroyed by a car accident. These people often use the accident (and alleged injuries) as a means of escape from their "lives of quiet desperation," to use Henry David Thoreau's phrase. They fixate on the accident and the lawsuit, and they attribute all their problems to the accident. As a result, they magnify their problems. Some experts have referred to this phenomenon as litigation neurosis.

## Responsible Parenting

The acceptance of responsibility also applies fully in the area of parenting. It is all too easy to blame problems with our children on television, peer pressure, modern music, lack of role models, and so on. The fact is that the primary role models for a child should be his or her mother and father. If we are not responsible for nurturing and raising up our children, who is? Right now the government is attempting to take over that role.

Too many parents depend on schools to teach attitudes and values to their kids. Many public schools,

41

however, can barely keep their students free from physical danger, let alone impart character and values to their students. In a large number of American schools, students are taught that there are no wrong or right attitudes or values; everything is relative, subjective, and malleable.

Elementary school children are put through the ringer of lifeboat exercises where children are forced to make decisions as to which children should be thrown overboard in order to save those remaining. Such exercises mislead children into thinking that every decision is a lifeboat decision with no real right or wrong answer; ethics and morality are situational. Therefore, decisions as to whether one should take drugs, have promiscuous sex, steal, lie, and cheat are all "lifeboat" decisions, impossible to measure from absolute and eternal standards. These school courses are often mischaracterized by names such as Sex Ed, AIDS Education, Values Clarification, Family Life, and Self-Esteem, though these programs often increase the severity of the very problems they are allegedly designed to cure.

Many Sex Ed courses focus on inane and inaccurate sloganeering about "safe sex." What sex educators call "safe sex" is nothing but a game of Russian roulette. Women frequently become pregnant—even when a condom is used—despite the fact that a woman is only fertile for a short time each month. However, a "death sentence" disease can be communicated—even when a condom is used—365 days per year. The irony of "safe sex" courses is that studies show that the result of these courses is even more promiscuity, disease, pregnancy, and abortion. To you and me, this might seem to be bad news. But for those who receive funding to allegedly "cure the problem" they created in the first place, it's good news. Of course, a great deal of the sex education propaganda emanates from Planned Parenthood, which profits from all of these problems that they cause in the first place.

Some Sex Education courses claim that they stress abstinence and safe sex simultaneously. Such conflicting messages, however, tend to confuse children rather than educate them; it's unequivocal messages that they truly need. True abstinence courses such as Leanna Benn's "Teen Aid" or Richard Panzer's "Free Teens" have produced tremendous results and have greatly decreased pregnancy and disease where they have been implemented.

Far from supporting such positive programs, Planned Parenthood and the American Civil Liberties Union are suing an abstinence course in Louisiana as we write this book. It turns out that teaching abstinence is viewed by these so-called civil liberties groups as tantamount to teaching the Bible. In other words, anything that is in the Bible cannot be taught to children even if religion and the Bible are not mentioned. Apparently, if someone in the Bible washes his hands before eating, we cannot tell a child that this is a good thing to do. My friends, the lunatics are running the asylum. And they talk about censorship!

Values clarification is a generic term encompassing the lifeboat methodology used in so many American schools. Its basic premise is that children have the right answers within them and do not need to rely on absolute standards set by their parents or church. The child is seen as Rousseau's "noble savage" uncorrupted by "instrumentalities of oppression" such as the Bible. Left to his own devices, the child will be able to clarify his values through logic, thought, and intuition. Representatives of values clarification programs such as Project Charlie say that "we teach children that all feelings are good." Such logic, carried to its extreme, would obviously conclude that Hitler had a "good feel-

43

ing" about the extermination of six million Jews, and Ted Bundy had a "good feeling" that caused him to cave in the skulls of dozens of women. For parents who want to find out why so many kids cannot tell the difference between right and wrong, we recommend a new book by Professor William Kilpatrick entitled *Why Johnny Can't Tell Right From Wrong.* This book is an invaluable tool in helping parents understand how their values are being undermined in the schools and how they must reinforce traditional values within *their* children.

The current fad in education is an obsession with self-esteem. Some educators no longer correct mistakes in spelling or reading for fear of injuring the child's self-esteem (they fail to anticipate the injury to the self-esteem of functional illiterates who are unable to make a living). The fact is that self-esteem is derived from accomplishment, not from walking around telling yourself how wonderful you are. Accomplishment is only achieved through the disciplined performing of unpleasant tasks.

A recent test compared Koreans to Americans. Both the Korean and American students were tested for self-esteem and math skills. The Koreans scored low in self-esteem and high in math. The Americans scored high in self-esteem and failed math—but they felt simply terrific about it. Parents, the bottom line is to take responsibility for giving your kids the right values. Produce self-esteem in your kids by showing them how applied discipline results in achievement.

There are essentially only two worldviews a person can have. One we will call a God-centered worldview and the other, a humanistic (not to be confused with humanitarian) worldview. A God-centered worldview is based on objective standards of absolute truth and absolute concepts of right and wrong. To someone with

44

a God-centered worldview, right and wrong is eternal. What is wrong today was wrong six thousand years ago and will be wrong years from now.

On the other hand, a humanistic worldview is subjective. Sometimes referred to as moral relativism, this worldview is based on the premise that right and wrong and truth are subject to the whims of mankind as times and moral standards change. Believe it or not, it is possible (but rare) for an atheist to have a God-centered worldview. It is also possible for a member of the clergy to be a humanist.

The values clarification programs are based on the humanistic worldview. They reflect a belief that individuals should not be taught that certain values are *objectively* right or wrong. Instead, they must be taught to look to themselves in order to find their own *subjective* values. Adolf Hitler was a humanist; he despised the Jews not only for bringing God's law to the world, but also for being the foundation of Christianity. Hitler, like Karl Marx and most modern liberals, believed in man's ability to create perfection, a master race. If only we could get rid of the unfit through abortion, sterilization, and murder, man could finally create the humanistic utopia he's searched for since the Garden of Eden.

Believe it or not, this philosophy has not only invaded the values aspect of education; subjective non-standards now dominate what's left of academic subjects in our nation's schools. Reading no longer entails being able to objectively decode what the writer has written. According to our "progressive educators," a word is anything the reader says it is. If the writer writes "the security guard was *uniformed*" but the reader reads "the security guard was *uninformed,*" that is good reading. In fact, to require a student to accurately read what is actually on the page is a form of political oppression, according to many professors of education.

45

How did we get into this mess of an education system?

In the 1800s, a man named Thomas Gallaudet came up with a method he hoped would be effective in teaching the deaf to read. It has been referred to over the years by various proponents as "look-say," whole language, whole word, etc. Gallaudet's technique had disappointing results among the deaf, yet it has come to be the method of choice for many of our nation's educators today.

What is this method? Why is it so pervasively used throughout America? One might ask the same question with regard to all the social programs of the past thirty years and get the same answer—the method is used precisely because it doesn't work!

Now, you may be asking, why would an entire system operate to perpetuate illiteracy? Well, why would a whole industry operate to perpetuate smoking? If you guessed "money" as the reason, you now qualify to teach reading methodology at your local teacher's college. Phonics books do not produce as much profit as whole language books because kids actually learn to read relatively quickly with phonics.

On the other hand, whole language publishers get to supply "reading" textbooks for years and then get to supply more books for the nonreaders they created in the first place.

Many of the reading professors at the various teaching colleges write the whole language reading books and, of course, require their students to purchase them. These students then go on to create "new illiterates" when they become teachers. In fact, we've created more than twenty million new illiterates who have gone to public school from eight to twelve years.

In other words, in order to be an illiterate you have to go to school—it's compulsory.

However, if you still don't believe this, listen to this quote from the legendary children's author, Dr. Seuss.

46

He told *Arizona Magazine* in 1981: "They think I did it in twenty minutes. . . . *Cat in the Hat* took nine months until I was satisfied. I did it for a textbook house and they sent me a word list. That was due to the Dewey revolt in the Twenties, in which they threw out phonics reading and went to word recognition, as if you're reading a Chinese pictograph instead of blending sounds of different letters. I think killing phonics was one of the greatest causes of illiteracy in the country. Anyway, they had it all worked out that a healthy child at the age of five can learn so many words in a week and that's all. So there were two hundred and twenty-three words to use in this book. I read the list three times and I almost went out of my head. I said, 'I'll read it once more and if I can find two words that rhyme, that'll be the title of my book.' (That's genius at work.) I found 'cat' and 'hat' and said, the title will be *The Cat in the Hat.*"

Rita Kramer has written another great book, *Ed School Follies—The Mis-Education of America's Teachers.* Rita Kramer attended most of America's major teacher's colleges in order to investigate why so many public schools are such utter failures.

Her first day at Columbia Teachers College is recounted in the book. One of the students in a lecture hall inquired of the professor, "What do you do when parents complain that their kids aren't learning phonics?" Without missing a beat, the professor responded facetiously, "We do teach phonics." This is exactly what happens to many parents when they question their school's reading program. They are assured by the school authorities that their kids are being taught phonics.

Recently Robert Sweet Jr., president of the National Right to Read Foundation, recounted to me an incident that is all too typical. Bob saw a flyer advertising a "Phonics" lecture being held at his local public school. Bob was elated with the hope that the schools were finally going to return to competency in teaching children to read. He attended the seminar and was horrified as the speaker gave a lecture based on whole language methods, not phonics. Bob felt like he was in the twilight zone, because the lecturer constantly referred to this whole language as phonics. Subsequently, Bob phoned this teacher and decided to be as "wise as a serpent, gentle as a dove." He complimented her excellent whole language presentation and asked her why she referred to it as "phonics." She responded matter of factly, "The parents want their kids to learn phonics, so we teach what we want and tell the parents that it's phonics."

If you think that's scary, a recent report issued by the Michigan State Senate reported that the education bureaucracy was holding seminars on how to deceive and discredit parents. They even went as far as to tell seminar participants that concerned parents should be publicly labeled Christians or Fundamentalists. The media has painted Christians as ignorant Nazis so much that, in many circles, labeling a parent as Christian is tantamount to discrediting the parent. A writer for the *Washington Post* recently referred to biblical Christians who are concerned about the moral relativism being taught in our schools as "poor, uneducated and easy to command." This opinion was not uttered in an editorial, but was presented as a statement of fact in a news story.

Recently co-author John Kupillas, in a local school board debate, referred to Bill Kilpatrick's book, *Why Johnny Can't Tell Right From Wrong,* in support of his opposition to the elementary school sex education course. Instantly, a teacher stood up and said, "I'm very disturbed by your referring to that book. Doesn't the

author come from a Catholic College?" The implication, of course, was that such a background would
somehow discredit the author and his book.

Co-author Bob Unger recently appeared on the
*Sonya Live* show on CNN to debate the proponents of
the "Rainbow Curriculum" of the New York City Public School System. The Rainbow Curriculum teacher's
guide told teachers that five- and six-year-olds are not
likely to bring up homosexuality, so it is incumbent
upon the teacher to unilaterally bring it up. The curriculum also contained the totally discredited Kinsey
claim that homosexuals comprise 10 percent of the
population (the real figure is 1 to 2 percent) and urged
the teachers to stress the "positive aspects" of homosexuality. Is that tolerance or advocacy? The curriculum also recommended books to be read by the class.
Some of the titles were *Daddy's Roommate* (which
shows daddy and his "roommate" lying together in
bed) and *Gloria Goes to Gay Pride* (wherein little Gloria repeats "two, four, six, eight, being gay is really
great"). Is that tolerance or advocacy?

What's next in our schools—bestiality, pedophilia,
or incest? A reading of *Why Johnny Can't Tell Right
From Wrong* will reveal that these things are already a
part of all too many schools' curriculae. We don't enjoy
telling you these facts, but before you can take positive steps to fight back, you must first know reality. Unfortunately, all too many parents are like ostriches:
their heads are in the sand.

Now let's get back to teaching our kids how to read.
Contrary to the whole language philosophy, English is
not a pictographic language like Chinese. The Phoeni-
cians invented the alphabet so that letters and their
various combinations would stand for specific sounds
(known as phonemes). There are forty-four phonemes
in the English language. Thus, one can learn to read

English simply by learning the phonemes and then blending them together to "sound out words." Simplicity and economy is the reason why phonics, for the most part, is kept out of public schools.

The bureaucrats and bogus scientists have even invented a mysterious learning disability/disease known as dyslexia. The bureaucrats and scientists then milk the public for money grants to study this mysterious rampaging epidemic! They claim that up to 20 percent of the population has this "brain problem," which causes its victims to reverse and mix up the order of letters in words.

In the 1930s, neurologist Dr. Samuel Orton reached the conclusion that whole language reading was creating dyslexics by impairing the neurological process required to sound out words. As Literacy Council Chairman Charles Richardson states, "A child tends to 'latch on' to what he learns first—he acquires what psychiatrists call a 'conditioned reflex.' Once in place, such a reflex is highly resistant to change. (Think of trying to drive on the left, as in England.)"

The overwhelming majority of cases of dyslexia constitute *teaching* disabilities, not learning disabilities. And so the whole language illiteracy creation goes on and on.

Parents, make sure your child is taught systematic intensive phonics (not eclectic or window dressing phonics, which combines some of the sounds of the alphabet with guessing of words from context and whole word memorization).

Bob Unger's children learned to read from "Hooked On Phonics." Many of you have heard their ubiquitous "just dial 1-800-ABCDEFG" commercials on radio and television. The story of John Shanahan and the "Hooked On Phonics" program's success is an example of how to teach reading—and an example of how a true entrepreneur becomes successful by seeing a need and then finding a way to fill that need.

Gateway Educational Products of Orange, California, makers of "Hooked On Phonics," came into being because CEO John Shanahan's youngest son was throwing up. He was literally scared sick of school, because he couldn't read. He couldn't read because he was never taught intensive systematic phonics.

John Shanahan had started a career as a piano player and composer. He came out to California to score motion pictures. Eventually, he left the music business and entered the advertising business, where he worked buying advertising time. Little did he know how these two prior careers would one day equip him to help millions of people learn how to read.

When John discovered that his son had never been taught phonics, he made up a cassette tape in order to teach his son the alphabetic code. Eventually, other parents heard about the tape and expressed interest in it for their children. Then John's musical and advertising background were put to entrepreneurial use. John developed a program based on combining the alphabetic code with music and rhythm. His advertising acumen told him to dial 800-ABCDEFG. When a businessman answered, John negotiated with the man to buy the 800 number from him since the ABCDEFG was not essential to that man's business. John then used his expertise in buying time to shrewdly purchase advertising at the best available times and rates. The rest is history.

One parent recently called our radio show to tell us that his son was using the "Hooked On Phonics" program at the same time that his dad was teaching him about "Noah's Ark." One day, the little boy just brought out the family Bible and began reading about "Noah's Ark" for himself. It doesn't get any better than that.

Another vital part of the war against illiteracy is the National Right to Read Foundation. NRRF President, Robert Sweet Jr., had previously been head of the Office of Juvenile Justice and Delinquency Prevention. When Bill Clinton was elected, Bob Sweet had to decide what he would do with the rest of his life. He had at one time been executive director of the National Council on Education Research, director of the National Institute of Education, and special assistant in the U.S. Department of Education. Having been involved in both education and juvenile delinquency prevention, Bob knew all too well the connection between the two areas. So Bob decided he would devote his life to seeing to it that we begin once again to teach children how to read in this country. As President of the NRRF, he is doing just that. The National Right To Read Foundation (800-468-8911) provides a national network to help the 90 million people who are either illiterate or minimally literate. In addition, it provides tutoring and a simple test which can tell parents whether their kids can really read, or, as in many cases, whether their kids have merely memorized enough words to read the simplest books.

NRRF is the only vehicle out there that can "circumvent the existing education macrostructure." When we say "existing education macrostructure" we are quoting a Blue Ribbon Committee on Reading that was appointed by the National Academy of Education in 1975. In its report, the Committee had this to say: "We believe that an effective national reading effort should bypass the existing education macrostructure. At a minimum, it should provide alternatives to that structure. That is, the planning, implementing, and discretionary powers of budgeting should not rest with those most likely to have a vested interest in maintaining the status quo, especially given their unpromising track record." In other words, the existing education bureaucracy does not care that there is a reading problem because they milk this problem which supplies money, jobs, and the perpetuation of programs for the bureaucracy. The NRRF mission is to educate parents, politicians, and maybe even teachers that the solution to the illiteracy problem simply lies in getting back to the basics. Intensive systematic phonics is the most important of the basics.

The great educational writer, Samuel Blumenfeld, commented on this National Academy of Education report by stating, "what the Committee was telling us in effect, is that the greatest obstacle to literacy in America is our own education establishment and that if we want to achieve real education in our country, we shall have to circumvent that establishment. What a staggering indictment. The system had been created to assure literacy for all. Now, we were being told that it was an obstacle. How could you circumvent $100 billion worth of educational malpractice?" Bob Unger's wife, Dr. Phyllis Unger, runs a learning center in Great Neck, New York. Most of her students have been labeled "learning disabled." She simply teaches them intensive systematic phonics and eventually they are all "cured."

Humanistic education is leading us up another Tower of Babel where we will deconstruct our language to the point where in-depth communication with each other becomes impossible. As a result, our history and culture will be Balkanized and will not be passed on to our children.

The great writer, George Orwell, in his classic book, *1984*, warned that when Newspeak (language without objective meaning) replaces Oldspeak (accurate objective meaning) in-depth thoughts will become impossible, because we cannot think without words. We still have time to turn this around. Act today to save tomorrow.

53

Take responsibility for properly educating your own kids. Then do what you can to help educate other kids.

In essence, schools have become institutions of indoctrination, not education. The "three Rs" have been replaced by political and sociological brainwashing. Schools have been turned into social laboratories with our children as the guinea pigs. Children are made to sit around in circles discussing their feelings with teachers practicing psychotherapy without a license.

The icons of western civilization like Christopher Columbus are trashed while third world cultures that engage in human sacrifice are exalted.

Radical environmentalism is force fed to the kids everyday. The radical environmentalist movement deifies the earth and makes no distinction between human and animal life. These people would experiment on humans in order to find cures for laboratory rats; unborn human babies have no right to life, but baby seals and whales elicit campaigns of heartfelt support.

The schools present global warming, population bombs, and their disproven fantasies as fact, not theory. That is why parents must educate themselves before they can educate their children. Turn off the boob tube and read every night. You'll be surprised at how well informed you become. For example, did you know that the same people who claim that the earth is warming predicted an ice age just twenty years ago? Yet, few people bother to question their credibility. Did you know that the "ozone hole" over Antarctica was observed by French scientists (and by Gordon Dobson) in 1956, years before CFCs were widely used? Did you know that NASA's Numbus satellite data showed no global warming trends in the 1980s at all? Did you know that a federal government study known as NAPAP has revealed that acid rain is not a serious environmental hazard; very few lakes and virtually no forests are being affected by this supposed hazard? Did you know that three volcanos (Mt. St. Helens in Washington, Krakatoa in Indonesia, and Heckla in Iceland) have released more pollutants into the atmosphere than all of man's activities since the beginning of time? Did you know that a minimum of two trees are planted for every one cut in the U.S.? Every day the forest industry, together with federal and state forestry agencies, plants over six million trees. Figures from the American Forest Council and the U.S. Forest Service prove that the United States has more trees today than it did seventy years ago! Did you know that Greenpeace has found that only 13 percent of atmospheric scientists actually think there is a strong possibility that we are experiencing a global warming trend? Did you know that scientists expressing doubt about global warming amount to about 70 percent of those polled by S. Fred Singer's Science & Policy Project (Washington, D.C.)?

The following books are suggested for learning the truth about environmental issues so you can counter the "green" propaganda: *The War Against Population: The Economics and Ideology of Population Control* by Jacqueline Kasun, Ignatious Press, 1988; *Trashing the Planet* by Dixy Lee Ray and Louis R. Guzzo, Regnery Gateway, 1990; *The Ultimate Resource* and *Population Matters* by Julian Simon, Transaction Publications and Princeton University Press, respectively; *The Resourceful Earth* by Julian Simon and Herman Kahn, Basil Blackwell, 1984; and *Why Are They Lying to Our Children?* by Herbert London, Stein and Day, 1984.

In reality, radical environmentalism is a vehicle for the socialists and other America haters to attack our free enterprise system. This is clever strategy on their part because no one wants to be accused of not "caring" about our environment.

Unfortunately, parents cannot always rely on school boards or the PTA. School boards and PTAs are supposed to be watchdogs for parents and students. However, in all too many cases, they are lapdogs for the education establishment. They even lobby and implicitly threaten school children to get their parents to pass school budgets. The following letter was sent to Bob Unger's five- and eight-year-old by the PTA:

Dear Kids,

Just a short note to tell you about the budget. A group of concerned people including parents, members of the Board of Education and administrators, work very hard to plan for next year's school budget. The budget describes how our monies are distributed to pay for the things we need. It includes furniture, books, pencils, computers, teachers and everything else that makes your school run smoothly. After the plan is made, it goes to the public for a vote. Who votes? Parents, grandparents and all people who pay taxes and live in Great Neck.

However, some taxpayers who do not have kids in school vote *against* the budget without really knowing how this hurts YOU KIDS. Activities like intramural sports, summer programs, additional bus service, cultural arts, and many other special programs could no longer be available if the budget is NOT passed.

Please mark your school calendar Wednesday May 12th and remind your parents to vote *"YES"* for the school budget.

School children are being taught how to vote in favor of more and more government intrusion. The *Wall Street Journal* recently reported that school kids are being monitored electronically by the administration to make sure they are becoming "good citizens" (real robots who will support more taxes and government control). In *Educating For the New World Order,* Beverly Eakman (Halcyon House), explains how a major tax-exempt foundation influences American education; the extent to which assessment tests measure students' attitudes rather than achievement; how the schools are being used as instruments of change to reshape the way children think; how personal information on individuals and families is being compiled and stored in non-secure data banks; how parents can be stonewalled by the education bureaucracy; why teachers are unwitting pawns of the establishment; why remedial reading has become institutionalized and why efforts to reform education have failed.

My friends, "Big Brother" is upon us. Hopefully this book will serve as your wakeup call. Your children are not government property. Do not allow your rights as parents to be usurped. Take responsibility for informing yourself, your family, your friends, and neighbors. Above all, take full responsibility for your child's education. If you don't, the education bureaucracy will.

## Taking Responsibility Fosters Self-esteem

Your level of self-esteem is always based on the degree of control you are able to exercise over yourself, and thus over your life. People with low self-esteem are people who do not believe that they have any power over, or *responsibility* for, their lives. They are the perennial victims and martyrs. They are leaves tossed by the winds of chance blown about with any sudden change in the weather.

You can exercise control over your life only to the degree that you believe *you* are responsible for the direction of your life. Failures think that everything happens by accident and chance. Successful people realize that they are responsible. Everything happens as a result of something. If we can identify the cause, we can control the effect.

*We* are responsible for what we *choose* to *think* and *believe.* As the Bible says, "As a man thinketh in his heart, so is he."

We know that one generally rises to the level that one expects. *We* are responsible for setting our expectations.

We know that one's success is dependent upon one's level of confidence. *We* are responsible for thinking confidently about ourselves and the attainment of our goals.

We know that our attitudes and actions are a result of habits ingrained in us over a period of time. *We* are responsible for either reinforcing good habits or unlearning bad habits and consciously replacing them with consistently practiced good habits.

We also know that the power of suggestion is very strong, and that "birds of a feather flock together." *We* are responsible for *choosing* to associate with positive people. *We* are responsible for finding, planting, and nurturing the seeds that contain future victory, born from setbacks.

In short, in all the areas of your life—financial, physical, emotional, or spiritual—*you* are responsible. Once you recognize this, accept it, and firmly believe it, you are on the road to success. If you fail to accept this basic tenet, no success system or formula will pull you out of the hole *you* have dug for yourself.

Acceptance of responsibility is the crucial starting point of a successful life. None of the practical techniques for achievement are of value unless you first realize that you can take control of your life. You will not set a definite written goal, with a plan for its attainment on a certain date, unless you realize that you will take control of your life by doing so. If you believe that you are totally controlled by fate, your environment, or other external forces, then you most certainly will be ruled by those forces. All causation is mental, and you can control your thoughts. It's up to you to use the abilities God has given to you and the opportunities he has opened to you to make your future all it can be.

# 2

# GOALS

*You'll Get There
if You Know Where You're Going*

## Why We Must Have Goals

You can't get there if you don't know where the heck you're going. Does this sound too obvious, like something anybody would know? Well, obvious or not, we have 95 percent of the population walking, driving, or flying through life without the foggiest notion of where they are aiming to go. They have no destination. The unfortunate truth is that most people never set themselves a definite, meaningful goal. They are like ships without a rudder, subject to every wind and current. All too often they wind up shipwrecked for life.

You must have a goal—a definite, desired end that consumes you, gives meaning and direction to your life, gives you a raison d'être, a reason for living. A goal works like a magnet, and its magnetic force will pull you to success and fulfillment. Isn't it a lot easier to get to the corner store if you know where it is? If you know the store is on Main Street and Canal, it's easy to plot the course that will get you there. But how could you ever get there if you don't know where you are going?

Moreover, if you don't have a goal, how do you know when you have succeeded? That is, how will you know you've arrived at the place you are trying to go? Goals are the only way to measure what we've done. Every study of successful individuals shows that goal-setting played a vital role in their success. Perhaps the most telling study was performed at Yale University with a 1950s graduating class. The survey found that only 3 percent of the class had written goals for the future. The same class was surveyed again some twenty-five years later. The results were astonishing. The 3 percent who had written down their goals had amassed over 90 percent of the group's wealth. In addition, they seemed happier and better adjusted. What a dramatic example of the power of goal-setting!

## What Do You Really Want?

The most common "but" that we encounter in response to our directive to go out and find a goal is, "But I just don't know what I want." People who "just don't know what they want" are people who just don't follow Socrates' advice to "know thyself."

Most people spend a large part of their lives running away from themselves. They are afraid to stop, even for an instant, and look into that figurative mirror. They are afraid they may not like what they see. This is true not only with regard to the way people view themselves but also how they view those close to them. Many marriages have shattered because of wishful viewing of prospective mates during courtship, seeing them not as they truly are but as they are hoped or wished to be.

How many times have you observed a teenager following the destructive path of drug or alcohol abuse right under the nose of his parents? Somehow, his parents just don't seem to notice (or want to notice) what is so obvious from an objective vantage point. The parents have their heads in the sand, like ostriches.

We are all ostriches until we muster the courage to face the truth about ourselves and those we care about. So take your head out of the sand; the truth will set you free to change your bad habits, improve upon your good traits, and set a goal for your life.

It takes a great deal of courage to stop dead in your tracks and see yourself as you really are, warts and all. It takes courage to admit that wherever and whatever you are is the result of your own doing. It takes courage and causes pain. However, this courage and temporary sacrifice will one day lead to great progress. Once you have faced up to who and what you are, you can decide who and what you desire to become. The following poem is borrowed from materials prepared by Success Motivation Institute of Waco, Texas, materials we heartily recommend.

Your Competitor in the Day-by-Day Contest—Yourself

An enemy I had, whose face I stoutly strove to know.
For hard he dogged my steps unseen, wherever I did go.
My plans he balked, my aims he foiled, he blocked my
   onward way.
When for some lofty goal I toiled, he grimly said me,
   "Nay."
One night I seized and held him fast, from him the
   veil did draw, I looked upon his face at last, and
   lo—MYSELF I saw.

Take solace in the fact that you are the sum total of habits ingrained within you cumulatively right up to

63

the present moment. If you have the ability to develop a ton of bad habits, you can call upon the same ability to adopt new, good habits.

It has been found that a habit can be created in a brief period of time—usually several weeks. So you have the ability to replace your old bad habits with consciously created good ones in very short order. Some refer to this as the theory of displacement. Think of your bad habits as negatively charged water molecules filling a barrel to the top. If you pour positively charged water molecules into the barrel, the positive water will displace the negative water molecules. In the same way, you can displace your old, unproductive behavior patterns with new, better patterns and become, in effect, reborn.

Your mind is just like a computer programmed for success from birth. Feed positive software programs into that computer and you will succeed at being a success! Fill your "computer directory" with negative software programs, and you will "succeed" at being a failure!

## Why People Don't Set Goals

Why is it that people don't program goals into their lives? We have broken the answer down into seven categories, each a dangerous roadblock to effective goal-setting.

### Lack of Effort

Goal-setting requires effort. It is hard work to examine your life and then decide what you want to do with it.

George Bernard Shaw once remarked that he earned tremendous sums of money just for doing something a few times a week that most people never do: thinking. Perhaps he was right; many people seem to make every effort to avoid thinking.

Goal-setting requires thinking—hard thinking. And it is far better to think now than to agonize later.

Setting goals frees you to battle what we call negative inertia. Inertia is basically a physical law discovered by Sir Isaac Newton. The law states that any physical body persists in a state of rest or motion until acted upon by some external force.

Negative inertia is that state which exists when you take no action either to set goals or to carry them forward. Thus, you will continue on a stationary path to nowhere. You become, as the Beatles wrote in their hit song, "a real nowhere man." On the other hand, once you start setting goals, you begin to generate positive inertia. You become a snowball running down a snow-covered mountain slope, constantly picking up volume and velocity.

## Fear of Failure

Fear of failure may be the most common roadblock to goal-setting. People refuse to set goals because they fear that by setting a goal they, and others, will be able to determine whether they have succeeded. They are afraid of what others may think of them, and they are afraid of what they may think of themselves. People who fear failure live by the maxim, "If you don't try, you can't fail." They conveniently gloss over the most important maxim: "You can't succeed if you don't try." When H. Ross Perot attempted to fly to North Vietnam to give needed supplies and comfort to American POWs, he was callously turned away by the Communists. When the media referred to his aborted mission as a failure, he was quick to point out that he did not fail—*he did not fail to try!*

People who fear failure are outwardly driven; their actions are based upon external factors. They allow

65

other people and circumstances to dictate the terms of their life. They are adversely influenced when others say "You can't do it." They fail to recognize that when someone says "You can't do it," he is merely projecting his own limitations onto them.

Winners do not assume that what is true for others applies to them. They recognize that others will always view them from the confines of their own limited perspective and experience. They are inner-directed; they take their cues on how to think, act, and feel from an inner voice. They have come to rely upon that inner voice.

Another root cause of the fear of failure is fear of rejection. Quite often, people who fear failure have parents who responded to their childhood dreams with a "you can't" attitude. Each time her parents react negatively to her expressed desires, the child becomes increasingly hesitant to express those desires. Eventually hesitancy to express desire becomes hesitancy to desire.

Parents can also instill fear of failure in a child by inadvertently making the child think that the parents' love depends on the child's success. This is known as conditional love. The child comes to fear that if he does not receive high grades in school, he will be denied his parents' love. This type of fear can be devastating to a child and can have paralyzing aftereffects.

Conditional love and high demands should not be confused with high expectations. Having high expectations for children usually leads to the child's fulfilling those expectations. People generally rise to meet positive expectations.

When we were making the important decision of whether or not to leave our "secure" jobs as lawyers in an established firm with a thriving practice, we were afraid of failing. What if we couldn't attract our own clients? What if we didn't get any cases? How would we pay the rent? Our fears were only reinforced when we spoke to others. Many established lawyers told us, "You're making a big mistake, this is a bad time to start a practice, you'll starve!"

We were fortunate to meet one wise old-timer, Manny Maisel, who gave two gloomy singing lawyers some sound advice. We asked him what would happen if we did not succeed. The old sage said, "They'll line both of you up before a firing squad, that's what will happen!"

This facetious statement instantly put everything in proper perspective. In reality, nothing would happen. If we didn't succeed, we would have to get another job. Big deal!

Fear is not a natural state of the human species. God made us for faith, not fear. Just as health (not disease) is a natural state, faith (not fear) is natural, too. In the immortal words of Franklin Roosevelt, "The only thing we have to fear is fear itself." Think of all the heroic veterans who risked their lives for us. Their courage in the face of death shows us how petty some of our fears really are. Their example should serve as the wind beneath our wings. Why should we be afraid to fly?

The choice to start our own firm seemed at the time like a monumental decision. It wasn't—not compared to really monumental decisions like the signing of the Declaration of Independence. That was literally a life-and-death decision. For those who signed, the risks were real. They risked a lot more than embarrassment. If they had not succeeded in their revolution against Great Britain, they would have faced a hangman's noose around their necks.

You can't succeed without failing. Thomas Edison failed thousands of times in his attempt to discover the electric lightbulb. Yet he kept his perspective. Edison told others that he hadn't failed at all. He had just discovered a few thousand ways how not to invent the electric lightbulb.

Winners don't view failures as failures. Rather, they consider so-called failures to be "learning experiences and opportunities." To them, there is no such thing as failure, only new discovery. Like a heat-seeking missile that continually corrects its course, winners always move steadily toward their goal, quickly correcting any deviations. The missile goes off course intermittently, but always gets back on target; so does the winner.

Sigmund Freud thought that goal-setting was potentially dangerous and advised against it. He said that setbacks would lead to disappointment, frustration, and unhappiness. He failed to realize that if setbacks were viewed as the positive learning experiences they are, there would be no frustration. The key lies in how you view an alleged setback. If you allow it to affect your faith adversely, then Freud's prophecy will be fulfilled.

Aristotle, contrary to Freud, said we are goal-seeking organisms. Our lives have meaning only when we are striving toward an objective. We side with Aristotle.

Who cares what others think? Why should you concern yourself with the opinions of others? Opinions, after all, are the cheapest commodities on earth. Just listen for a day to talk radio or watch a few hours of television talk shows, and you'll realize that opinions are as cheap as dirt. Remember, there are some people who will not like you no matter what you do. That's human nature. Even the most popular presidents have nearly 50 percent of the people voting against them. You might as well realize that when you achieve success, you will face a certain amount of jealousy and envy. When you join the top 5 percent of the population, some of the 95 percent who are not successful will be taking potshots at you. You can't do anything about this, nor should you try. Nor should you care; it's actually a great compliment.

If you can learn to dismiss the negative reactions of others, you then have to contend merely with your own reaction. If you view failure as a learning experience, you will try again and again. You will not fail. In the end, tenacity, not talent, determines success.

## *Fear of Success*

This fatal roadblock to goal-setting seems paradoxical at first glance. Yet it may be as common as fear of failure. Many of us have been brought up to believe it is somehow sinful to desire, let alone expect, to go beyond the norms of the masses and blaze one's own trail. People with low self-esteem are especially reluctant to depart from the status quo. Therefore, we strive to be like everybody else, to be average. Do you really want to be just average?

Another type of success-shy person is the one who commits acts in his life that are not in harmony with his concept of moral right and wrong. Later he represses all memory of these acts. The mind, however, never really forgets anything. As a result, he consistently sabotages himself every time he appears to be on the brink of success. This "death wish" occurs on a subconscious level. You may recall that when rumors arose about presidential contender Gary Hart's personal life, he actually invited the press to follow him around. Sure enough, the press caught him in a compromising situation. It was almost as if he was asking to have his presidential bid destroyed. Perhaps—on a subconscious level—he was.

Some who fear success are afraid that one success will place great pressure on them to repeat their success. As a result, they revert to the "fear of failure," assuming that if they remain in their present state, their lack of success will go unnoticed.

## Fear of Accepting Responsibility

As we said in the first chapter, if you do not believe that you have some control of your own destiny, you will never begin to set goals. Why would a leaf blowing in the wind think it can control the direction in which it is being blown? Only people with healthy self-esteem will set goals. It is no coincidence that people who don't feel they have the ability to control their own lives also lack the requisite self-esteem.

"Que será será, whatever will be will be" is the common theme of many people's lives. Because certain accidents, certain illnesses, deaths of loved ones, and the fluctuations of the stock market are beyond our control, we may be tempted to say that our entire life is beyond our control. This is the easy way out. If things are outside of our control, then why attempt to control them? It's easier to see what happens than to *make* things happen.

Many people believe that everything will work out all right. This may be true, but we don't want things to work out all right; we want things to work out great! For things to work out great, we must aim for greatness.

Some people believe that by setting goals they are interfering with God's eternal plan. Yet men and women of God provide vivid examples of goal-setting. The patriarch Joseph outlined a fourteen-year plan for Egyptian famine relief; Joshua set and accomplished detailed goals for the Israelite conquest of Canaan; the Israelites would have remained in subjection to Jabin and Sisera had Deborah not seized the initiative and obtained their deliverance; Jesus himself "steadfastly set his face to go to Jerusalem," a goal from which he never wavered.

If you believe that *you* have responsibility, you will take the steps necessary to set goals. Even if you don't

70

believe you control everything in your life, by setting goals you will certainly reduce the number of things you can't control. The truth is that you can control most things in your life. God has given us all a valuable freedom, freedom of *choice.* Choose to take control of your life; choose to decide just what you want; choose to set your goals. Choice, not chance, creates destiny.

## Fear of Rigidity

Many people think that having goals will trap them into a rigid lifestyle. They fear that they will lose their flexibility. Actually, the opposite is true. By setting goals, you focus your energy on specific items. Hence, you do not experience energy leaks. Once your goals are achieved, you will have more free time to perform extra tasks.

Failure to set goals is the real trap. Without goals you have no sense of where you are or where you are going. By directing your energy toward your goals, you free your mind and your time. When you have goals, you are able to make decisions faster, and thus you have more time to think. For every hour you spend setting goals, you save two hours of trying to figure out where you are and where you are going.

## The Right-Track Syndrome

Many people lack even the semblance of a goal. Others fudge it. They point themselves in the right direction. They get on the right track. But instead of taking the time to set specific goals, they just tread water, figuring that the current will carry them to success.

Those who take this route of compromise achieve compromised results. While the people on the right track are better off than drifters, they can't compete with

71

the goal-setting winner. In fact, the people on the right track (just like the drifters) end up working for the goal-setting winner.

Look at how many of the larger law firms and accounting firms work. Young professionals are told they are on the partnership track. In other words, someday—usually after seven years or more—if you work very hard, if your area of expertise doesn't decline, if partners are needed in your specialty, and if the head partners (mostly goal-setting winners) feel you are deserving, then, maybe, you will get some piece of the action.

People who work for these firms are certainly well paid, but often it's blood money. They must sacrifice their personal lives in order to serve the firm's clients. The small percentage who are made partners are often partners in name only. They have no real voice in how the firm is run. They make "good money" while the head partners get rich.

This phenomenon also occurs in the corporate world. A middle manager works for years in the corporation. He or she then climbs the corporate ladder, all the time staying on the right track. There comes a rude shock, however, when a goal-setting corporate raider leads a successful takeover of the corporation. Under new management, the right-track manager is likely to be let go.

The problem with getting on the right track is that there's a tendency to stop progressing. To the right-tracker, impetus comes from external, not internal sources. The next project—a superior's whim, or a midterm examination—dictates his actions. Then he's not much better off than the drifter. For the drifter, the wind blows in all directions. The right-tracker never knows when and with what velocity it will blow. Will Rogers said, "Even if you're on the right track, you'll get run over if you just sit there."

The right-track syndrome offers a false sense of security. This is why people flock to it—to obtain "security." However, there is no security in life, only opportunity. The risk-taking goal-setter will always receive many times the compensation of the security-seeking right-tracker, and rightfully so. Civilization leaps ahead on the shoulders of the leaders, not the followers.

## Fear of Change

Those who fear change will not set a goal because setting progressively higher goals pulls you out of what is most commonly referred to as the comfort zone. As the name implies, it refers to thoughts and actions with which you're comfortable.

Successful individuals constantly challenge themselves and stimulate their minds by venturing out of their comfort zone. As a result, each time they take on a new challenge, their comfort zone expands to encompass it.

Successful people welcome change because they understand that to accept change creates a healthy attitude. Life consists of constant change, and each change creates a new challenge that can stimulate you to adapt that change to your benefit. Increased self-esteem is the by-product of successful adaptation to change.

Those changes that are viewed by others as worrisome are really exciting new opportunities to venture out from the cocoon of the comfort zone. Welcome change into your life and, like Mohammed Ali, you will "float like a butterfly, sting like a bee." By setting goals, you will be the one creating the change; you will be in charge. Even if unanticipated problems arise, you will view them as exciting new opportunities to set goals.

It is only when we are progressively realizing worthy goals that we are engaged in the pursuit of happiness. So "Don't worry, be happy," and set a worthy goal.

Just what should your life's goal be? What would your goal be if God came to you and said, "You cannot fail"? The goal you would set for yourself under these circumstances is precisely the goal you should set for yourself today. You cannot fail!

All of us are born with a gift in at least one area. The only difference between a so-called genius and the rest of us is that the genius has discovered exactly what gift he has.

## Nine Rules of Goal Setting

### Rule 1:
### Write Down Your Goals—Talk Is Cheap

Anyone who has ever bought or sold a home probably knows that an oral agreement to buy or sell a house is as binding as "the check is in the mail." Until the oral statement is transformed into a signed written agreement, it has no binding effect. Whoever first conceived of the written contract—it must have been a lawyer—knew that it created more than a legal obligation. Putting something in writing somehow carries with it a moral dimension that cannot be matched by oral promises.

The vibrations of cheap talk are carried away by sound waves never to be heard from again. In contrast, something in writing solidifies a commitment. So make the most sacred contract with yourself: write out your goals.

Writing out a goal plants it deep into your subconscious. Your subconscious in turn guides you toward the thoughts, actions, and people you will require for the progressive realization of your written goals.

An example occurred in our lives when we wrote down some goals in 1985. Our least emphasized written goal that year was to sing the national anthem for the New York Mets and the New York Jets. After writing down this goal, we placed the piece of paper in a desk drawer.

As a result of not reviewing our goals even once in 1985, they slipped from our conscious (as opposed to subconscious) memory.

One morning in the spring of 1987, we received a phone call from Lee Rothleder, sales manager of the Schlott Realtors near our law office in Great Neck, New York. Lee asked us if we would like to meet Tommy Agee, of Sportsland Title Insurance Company and outfielder for the New York Mets in 1969, their first world championship year. Of course we asked him if he could arrange for us to sing the national anthem for the Mets at Shea Stadium. Did we sing it? Not only did we sing it, but we sang it for a capacity crowd occasioned by the comeback debut of pitcher Dwight Gooden!

In the winter of 1987, our good friend Ted Metalios, of Century 21 Metalios in Jackson Heights, Queens, sponsored a gala Sports Spectacular Salute to Easter Seals. Representative athletes from all the local New York metropolitan area sports teams attended the affair to promote the fine work of the Easter Seals organization. Ted Metalios, in his inimitable way as master salesman, induced us to purchase two tables and a full-page journal ad for the event. We, in *our* inimitable way, induced Ted to open the event with the Singing Lawyers performing the national anthem. We were introduced by comedian Freddy Roman.

After singing the national anthem, we approached a man from the Public Relations department of the New York Jets. The Jets were in the midst of a disappointing season. We knew they had three home games remaining: the first against the tough Miami Dolphins with all-pro quarterback Dan Marino; the next against the contending Indianapolis Colts, led by running superstar Eric Dickerson; the finale against the area rivals, the New York Giants. We audaciously promised the Jets that if they had the Singing Lawyers start off the games by singing the national anthem, the Jets would win every game. Did we make good on this promise? The answer lies in the following article, which is reprinted with permission of *New York Newsday*.

Oh Say You Can Win . . .

Two Great Neck lawyers, John Kupillas and Bob Unger, promised the Jets that they would win their last three home games if the team would let them begin the festivities by singing their harmonious version of the National Anthem. The Jets did. The Jets won. In fact, within the last 12 months, the Jets and the Mets have won at home each time the lawyers have sung the anthem. The lawyers, who are motivational experts, are 6-0.

"The Jets thought it was great," Unger told *Time-out*. "They got a big kick out of it."

Is this a coincidence? Luck?

Said Unger: "I don't think luck has the slightest thing to do with it."

Unger said it's simply locking into an unbeatable force created by the power of positive thinking (or positive singing). We harmonize parts of the song," he said. "We don't get away from it totally."

Unger said they wanted to sing for the Mets during the playoffs, but the team was booked. "And we know what happened to them in the playoffs."

In December of 1988, when we were preparing our written goals for the new year of 1989, we opened the desk drawer and stumbled across the piece of paper on which we had written down our goals for 1985. Sure enough, in black and white, was our goal to sing for the New York Mets and the New York Jets. Coincidence, some may say. We say, no way!

76

By writing out our 1985 goal of singing for the New York Jets and Mets, we allowed our subconscious mind to work toward the goal even though the goal had faded from our conscious memory.

When people tell us they don't have to write down their goals because they "have it in their mind," we know they are copping out. They really don't know or understand what their definite goal is. How often do you think you understand a concept, but when the time comes to express it in words, you are unable to do so? Anyone who has an idea or concept clearly defined should have no trouble expressing that thought in writing.

In order to obtain optimum results, don't just write down your goals once and then forget about them. Each morning when you get up, rewrite and reread your goals. Do it again just before retiring. To make sure you do this, keep your list of goals at your bedside.

While you are in the process of rewriting and rereading your goals, it is vital that you visualize yourself already in the possession of your goals, already the person you intend to become. This concept of visualization will be discussed later in greater detail. At this juncture, suffice it to say that just as writing your goals down stimulates your subconscious mind, simultaneous visualization of your intensely desired goals helps you mentally rehearse what you need to do to reach your goals.

Your goals must be crystal clear and detailed. Setting forth goals such as "I want to make a lot of money" or "I want to be happy" will not accomplish anything. If you want to own a luxury automobile, you must know every inch of that car in detail, replete with model, engine, size, color, material, and all other specifications. Your subconscious is not stimulated to action by vagaries. Details allow your mind to formulate a complete and vivid portrait of the life you want to live.

77

The difference between vague and definite goals can be illustrated by contrasting what you see through the lens of an out-of-focus camera as opposed to the appearance of a perfectly focused picture. Vague pictures of goals will give your mind vague instructions on how to obtain those goals. Clearly focused goals will drive the mind to find ways to carry you across the finish line.

## Rule 2:
## Prioritize Your Goals

All of us have conflicts of time and desire which we must resolve in order to clear a path to success. It is not uncommon to long for incompatible goals. For example, one cannot be a full-time, all-out career person and a full-time, all-out parent simultaneously. Some vehemently disagree with this statement, but they are just selling their own political agenda. As the song goes, "Something's gotta give." You *can* have it all, but you cannot have it all at the same time.

Our lives are made up of many segments. Because we are finite creatures confined by space and time, each area of life competes with another area. When we are at work, we miss our family. At home, our minds drift off toward those unfinished assignments. These competing and conflicting spheres in our lives can create anxiety unless we prioritize our lives in advance, and therefore avoid conflicts. This is exactly what people with stable lives do. They prioritize their household budgets, their work time, and their family time.

Any elected official who states he can simultaneously solve all the problems of this nation must be running for reelection or selling snake oil (maybe both). No government can put a "chicken in every pot." A wise leader knows that the goals of government must be prioritized in order to be effective.

Many of history's great leaders have been viewed as decisive, take-control individuals. It seems as if they never vacillate. What most people fail to realize is that the important decisions were made well in advance of the crisis that required a quick decision. Strong leaders have unshakable ideas and values. They know what they are for and they know what they are against. They have prioritized their goals and values. Therefore, when a conflict arises, they know what choice to make because they made that decision long ago.

Jimmy Carter was an extremely cerebral president who involved himself in great detail with the running of the presidency. Yet Carter was widely viewed as an ineffectual president. He seemed to tell the American people that they were in a state of national malaise. There was an implication that an American decline was practically preordained. In effect, Carter set a negative goal which, not surprisingly, led to negative results.

Along came Ronald Reagan with his simple, clearcut, deeply held values. He had a definite agenda. He reminded us that God had given human beings the free will to carve out their own destiny. When Reagan told us "America is back," we believed him. The American spirit was renewed and reaffirmed.

Ronald Reagan's values had been prioritized long before he entered the Oval Office. Molded by his small town of Dixon, Illinois, with its small-town values, he had a very clear sense of his priorities. He saw problems in terms of basic concepts of right and wrong. He had a God-centered worldview. Reagan's decision-making process was exemplified when he ordered the U.S. military to intercept a jet with terrorist murderers aboard. Various news stories carried a description of how the decision evolved. Reagan quickly gathered information from an assembly of experts. He asked them the "what if" questions and listened quietly to their answers. Then, as easily as most people choose food from a menu, he ordered the military operation to take place.

Write down your life's goals in the order of their priority. Make your decision in advance, so that when a conflict in goals arises you will not need to agonize over your decision.

Prioritization should be an ongoing process. It is inevitable that as you change, so will your priorities. Adapt to your personal growth by constantly reordering your goals in terms of their relative importance to you. As the great Sammy Cahn lyric reads, "You can be either read to or be the reader,/You can be either led or be a leader." Why not be a leader?

Once in a while, you may even be able to arrive at a compromise between conflicting goals. For example, many times as attorneys, both of us have to work on weekends. When we work on weekends, we miss our kids. We often solve this dilemma by bringing our kids to the office with us. They can color and write in the office just as easily as they can at home.

## Rule 3:
## Personalize Your Goals

Your goals must be just that: *your* goals—not your parents' goals, not your mate's, not society's. You will never be psyched to achieve someone else's goal. High achievement entails paying the price of forgoing immediate gratification and making many other sacrifices. How can one be driven to pay this high toll to get onto someone else's highway to success? Once again, it is the inner-directed individual who will be able to choose his goal, as opposed to the goals of those around him.

Many a midlife crisis has been brought on because a person was pushed into a career by others. Some hard-working, disciplined individuals reach a modicum of success in a field they do not enjoy. Eventually, however, their self-esteem diminishes. They suffer from the feeling of being powerless in their life, and their loved ones often suffer with them. You must do what you enjoy or make what you do enjoyable. How to make what you do enjoyable is discussed in the next chapter. Suffice it to say here that if you can neither enjoy what you do nor make what you do enjoyable, you should get out of your job as fast as you can.

Some people scurry all over the lot looking for something of value to do. Unfortunately, they never bother to look in their own backyard. Countless stories have been told of men digging for gold or drilling for oil who, after not quickly striking it rich, sold their drilling rigs and equipment to the first buyer for two cents on the dollar. The new owner dug one foot deeper and hit pay dirt.

Ted Metalios, of Century 21 Metalios, originally rented the lower portion of his home to a barber. Being totally bald, Ted eventually decided that he didn't really need a barber. He replaced the barber shop with his own little one-man/one-woman income tax office. Ted and his wife Mel were not CPAs, but Ted had learned a great deal by doing tax returns for friends and relatives.

Jackson Heights was and is a middle-class neighborhood with a rich diversity of ethnic groups. These people sometimes work two or three jobs at a time in search of the American dream.

Ted and Mel toyed with the idea of opening a real estate office because they foresaw that these hard workers could use real estate as both an income tax shelter and as an investment. They understood that real estate is the only investment that simultaneously depreciates for tax-shelter purposes, and appreciates for wealth-building purposes. The nay-sayers told Ted and

Mel that Jackson Heights was not conducive to building a large brokerage. They said that interest rates on mortgages were too high. Ted and Mel turned a deaf ear to the doubters and listened to their inner voice. They opened a mom-and-pop real estate office. Together, Ted and Mel drilled deep into a little Jackson Heights oil well and came up with a gusher. Against their lawyer's vehement advice—they hadn't met the Singing Lawyers yet—Ted and Mel decided to buy a Century 21 franchise. The rest is history. Since 1981, they have been the top residential real estate office in New York. Since 1985, they have been the top residential real estate office in the entire Century 21 U.S.A. territory.

## Rule 4:
## Set "Realistic" Goals, Not Low Goals

It's unrealistic for a man without an arm to pitch in the major leagues; but don't ask Jim Abbott.

It's unrealistic for a 5'5" man to ever conceive of playing in the NBA; but don't ask Spudd Webb.

It's unrealistic for an African-American to rise to the highest levels of the federal government; but don't ask General Colin Powell, former chairman of the Joint Chiefs of Staff.

It's unrealistic for a young man whose foot and part of his leg were cut off in an accident to run the hundred-meter dash in eleven seconds; but don't ask Dennis Oehler of Long Island, New York.

And it's unrealistic for a quadriplegic to think he can lead a productive life; but don't ask Walter Shinaut, Easter Seals representative for 1989. Walter severed his spine while in college. At first it was "unrealistic" of him to expect to live. Then he set the "unrealistic" goal of returning to college. In six months, the doctors were impressed by but concerned about his "unrealistic" optimism. Was he unrealistic? He was back at college within six months and today is a successful financial consultant. Walter enters information into all of his computers via a mouth stick and consults with his clients through the use of headphones. He has now set the unrealistic goal of building his own home and being financially independent by age forty-five. We wouldn't bet against him.

Setting a goal that is too low is far riskier than setting an "unrealistic" goal. If you set a low goal, you run the risk that you will never be motivated to try to attain it. You will not be motivated to obtain a goal that does not inspire you. Furthermore, even its attainment will, by definition, produce small results.

Trust your mind's intuition or inner voice and go with it. It is probably a more reliable barometer than your so-called rational thoughts. Rational thinking is greatly affected by your fears and by the opinions of others. Have faith that your mind will never allow you to visualize yourself already in possession of a goal that you are not capable of achieving.

## Rule 5:
## Get What You Need

Don't be a pipe dreamer. Bob recalls that as a kid he stood on a street corner talking to an illiterate loafer who was bragging about one day becoming head of a big company. Even then, Bob knew enough to suggest he first learn how to read and write. Unfortunately, Bob didn't know enough to avoid the left hook he got in reply.

Becoming the person you want to be requires intense development through hard work. First, you must visualize your model person, in great detail, taking note of each of the characteristics that enabled him or her to obtain that position. You must then embark upon a course to develop those same characteristics. This is called "modeling." This doesn't mean that you should become a clone. We all have our unique personalities and gifts. However, it is incumbent upon you, through the use of objective observation, to discern exactly what abilities and traits are required for the position you seek.

As a young teenager, Bob decided to become a professional singer. He had one slight problem, however; he didn't have professional singing ability. Even with today's music and modern studio techniques of electrically synthesizing sound, it certainly helps to have some talent. Bob set out to develop his. What the general public perceives as talent is very often the result of hard work and discipline. Bob found Jim Lynn, an absolute genius of a voice teacher located in New York City. Jim provided the exercises and techniques necessary for the building of the vocal instrument; Bob provided the belief and persistence. He vocalized for at least one hour each day, wherever he could. He vocalized in his car and at red lights, where he received many odd glances. When he vocalized in his apartment, the neighbors frequently banged on the pipes. He would yell back that they were lucky he wasn't charging them for the privilege of listening to his melodious golden notes. Bob even resorted to vocalizing in the woods at a summer bungalow colony in the Catskills, where residents feared what they thought was a pack of wolves.

Of course, in order to be a singing lawyer you also need to get a law degree and pass the bar exam. Bob and John both attended Fordham Law School. There they planted the seeds that eventually led to this book. Bob Unger told John Kupillas that passing the bar exam was not enough; he had to take voice lessons with Jim Lynn, too.

It may be necessary to tax yourself to the limit while you are in the process of laying the foundation for the future you. Go to any restaurant in the theater district and you will see budding actors and actresses working their feet off at night so they can take acting courses and audition during the day. You will find many a future lawyer or doctor behind the wheel of a cab working his way toward his goal. The Singing Lawyers worked at a multitude of jobs, including those of waiter, cab driver, garment cart pusher, and parking lot attendant. Bob Unger would come into Monday morning law classes at Fordham bleary-eyed after a Sunday night singing engagement that got him home at three o'clock in the morning.

Comedy superstar Joan Rivers worked at every job she could—as a clerk typist, receptionist, or whatever else it took—to enable her to make phone calls and run back and forth to auditions. Her story epitomizes the power of goal-setting, faith, and determination.

You will know instinctively when you are ready to be that person you want to be. Of course, even then, you will never stop learning and growing, because learning and growing are the essence of a productive life.

## *Rule 6:*
## *Phrase Goals in Positive Language*

Always phrase your goals in positive language. For example, if your goal is to live a healthy lifestyle, write "I will eat cholesterol-free foods" instead of "I will *not* eat foods with cholesterol in them." The mind works on the pictures you place in it. Although it has great trouble picturing you *not* doing something, it can easily picture you in the act of doing something.

If you were a golfer with a water hazard between you and the eighteenth hole, a positively phrased goal would be, "I will hit the ball over the water," as opposed to "I will not hit the ball in the water." If you use the first phrasing for your goal, your mind can visualize the ball's trajectory rising over the water. However, if you use the latter phrasing, your mind can't picture *not* hitting the ball in the water. It will picture hitting the ball and it will picture "in the water," and that is just where your ball may wind up.

## Rule 7:
## Set a Deadline

As the song goes, "Forget about tomorrow 'cause tomorrow never comes." Procrastination, akin to that negative inertia we spoke of earlier, is a major stumbling block for most people. The remedy for procrastination lies in setting a definite deadline for the attainment of your goals. Doing this will get your adrenaline flowing. It will overcome your negative inertia and force you to "do it now."

Watch any sporting event. A football game is played for sixty minutes; a baseball game runs nine innings; a boxing match goes ten, twelve, or fifteen rounds. You will often find that a team or player is lethargic for almost an entire game, when all of a sudden, with two outs in the ninth, there is an explosion of scoring. With three minutes to go in the Super Bowl, Joe Montana takes his team eighty-five yards to score the winning touchdown. These athletes know that they can coast for only so long. Otherwise the predetermined deadline will be upon them.

Set written deadlines for each of your goals. If by chance you don't reach the goal on time, don't commit suicide. Maybe your original deadline was unrealistic. Just set another deadline and keep going. This will drive you to get started today. Tomorrow may never come; tomorrow is just a promissory note. It is all too common for people to tell us, "If only I had started ten years earlier, but it is too late now." It is never too late, of course, but don't use that as an excuse to procrastinate. Set a deadline, and start working now to meet it.

## Rule 8:
## Set Goals Consistent with Your Values

Your goals must always be compatible with your underlying principles: you cannot be successful striving for aims that go against the grain of your concept of right and wrong, important and unimportant. Think of the foul lines of a baseball diamond as being the outside parameters of where you can safely travel on the field of success. It is only when you act within your value boundaries that you are truly successful, because moral conduct leads to self-respect. Immoral conduct leads to breakdown of self-respect and thus to lack of true success. In recent years we have witnessed a great number of scandals from Wall Street to the Congress. In their search for a quick buck and an easy way out, those involved have sacrificed their moral worth and self-respect. One allegedly corrupt New York City borough president dragged his self-respect down to the point where he was driven to plunge a knife through his heart.

Rotary International, of which both of us are members, has developed a four-way litmus test for business and social morality. The test asks:

1. Is it the **TRUTH**?
2. Is it **FAIR** to all concerned?
3. Will it build **GOODWILL** and better friendships?
4. Will it be **BENEFICIAL** to all concerned?

Define your fundamental values in writing and in order of their priority. You can match them up with your goals and see if they are consistent with each other. By doing this, you give purpose to your life. You understand exactly why you have set a specific goal, and this gives you an even greater reason to attain that goal. You will begin to zero in on those activities that promote your underlying principles. As a result, it will become easier to weed out those activities that do not reinforce your values, and you will be able to work more efficiently toward your goals.

## Rule 9:
## Practice Goal-Setting

Start setting long-term, ten-year, five-year, one-year, one-month, one-week, and one-day goals. Make sure that each of the shorter-term goals is somehow consistent with your longer-term goals. For example, let us say your goal is to become the president of the United States. It is difficult today to be the president of the United States if you are destitute. Therefore, an effective five- or ten-year intermediate goal might be to earn a specific amount of money. Remember, the amount must be specific because hazy aims cannot be visualized. You would then set a first-year goal of earning a specific amount of money. Meanwhile, you could set out to join organizations that would help you develop customers for your business and develop a network of future political contacts. Your daily, weekly, and monthly goals would then consist of doing things that moved you toward that larger goal.

Practice goal-setting daily. Start out with basics. You cannot get to the White House in one day. Each day, before you go to sleep, write out your "must do" list of goals for the next day, in the order of their priority. When the next day arrives, turn to that list and hit 'em out of the ballpark one by one. Success and failure are simply habits. Get in the habit of consistently setting goals and hitting the mark every day.

## To Tell or Not to Tell Others

Many great minds have differed on the issue of whether you should tell others about your big goals. Teddy Roosevelt felt that if he let it be known that he desired the presidency, it would result in the unleashing of all types of forces against him.

Those who agree with Roosevelt feel that you are surrounded by negative thinkers who will contaminate you if you tell them your positive goals. This, in turn, will generate fear and doubt within you about your ability to attain the goal. Furthermore, you will not want to incur the disapproval of your negative friends and relatives, so you will shrink from taking the necessary action to attain your goal.

Another school of thought is that the person who succeeds is the one who has the guts to shout his goals to the world. Each time he tells others about what he is going to do, he reaffirms the goal deeply within himself. Revealing the goals helps to battle procrastination, for failure to take action will not only be known by him but by all whom he has told. Therefore, if he does not take action to attain his goal, they will know that he was merely blowing smoke. His public image will suffer.

Revealing your goals may be vitally important and effective if you are the unusual person who is totally insulated from the influence of negative thinkers. Insulation can occur only if you limit your association to carefully chosen individuals who share your philosophy (remember, we are talking about less than 5 percent of the population). By sharing your aspirations with these people whose respect you have cultivated, you will gain the sum total of the group's energy and power. This will be a great aid in moving you toward the attainment of your goals. These fellow winners will rally behind you like an advancing army.

We have taken the position that early on in the development of your goal-setting ability, you probably will not yet have acquired your mastermind support group. Therefore, only those unusual individuals who, from the onset, are impervious to the doubts and scorn of negative people should risk publicly revealing their life goals.

## Everyone Is Motivated by the Right Goal

You often hear the remark, "I'm just not a motivated type of person." This is sheer nonsense. We are all motivated people; most of us just haven't set a worthy goal.

In 1989 our country experienced one of the few uprisings of the electorate in recent political history. For a long time American voters had been largely unmotivated and docile; we see this in the reelection of incumbent Congressmen at a 99 percent rate. As a result, these politicians grew increasingly brazen in their disregard for the electorate. This utter disregard led to a sneaky, back-alley attempt by Congress to vote itself an outrageous 50 percent pay raise. Congress was convinced that once again the ignorant and apathetic electorate would take it lying down. But, egged on by radio talk show hosts, voters mailed tea bags to their congressmen. This symbolic act served as a reminder that a new American revolution could result in the overthrowing of the greedy Congress. As you can see, the voters were finally motivated by a worthy goal, namely, saving themselves from being fleeced. Don't allow yourself to be fleeced out of life's unlimited opportunities for fulfillment; set a worthy goal.

Do not confuse setting a goal with reaching the goal. Focus on the goal first, not the difficulty in attaining it (attainment of goals will be further discussed in the next chapter). Many people get so caught up with the trivial problems of everyday striving that they lose sight of the goal itself. Move toward your goals the way a football running back makes a goal-line plunge into the end zone. As the opposing tacklers grab your legs and try to drag you down, keep your eye constantly fixed on that goal line—keep your eye on the prize. It's yours for the taking.

As we said earlier, always set new goals as you achieve old ones. This is what will give purpose and meaning to your life.

The friend of a successful man once told him, "I hope that you reach all of your goals before you die." The man replied, "But that would mean I had died before I died." Really live life; set your own personal, written, lofty, prioritized, positive, principled goals. Make yourself that person you long to see in the mirror. You can do it!

# 3

# PLANNING

*If You Fail to Plan, You Plan to Fail*

Now that you have established a specific written goal, you must create a step-by-step blueprint for attaining it. A plan is a logical working system for achieving a goal. A plan helps you to do more than just dream; we all have dreams. A plan will be your vehicle for action, another vital key to success. A plan will take your dreams from the intangible to the tangible, from the abstract to the concrete. A plan is a means by which you can map out the rest of your life right before your eyes like a screenwriter or director. In fact, the famous director Alfred Hitchcock was heard to say that by the time he actually began to direct the movie, all he had to do was go through the motions. He had already mapped out the movie well in advance of the actual filming.

## You Need a Plan

Just as a football team has a game plan and an army a battle plan, you must have a plan for achieving your goal. The creation of a systematic plan for achieving your goals is vital in the process of getting you to your goal line. Even if you have a written goal, it will be difficult to achieve it without a well-thought-out plan.

It is simply amazing that people will spend hours planning all sorts of trivialities but will spend very little time planning their lives. Studies have shown that people spend far more time researching and planning the purchase of a kitchen appliance, such as a microwave oven, than they do planning their financial investments. One reason is that many people feel overwhelmed by any attempt to plan the important things. It's safe enough to choose a kitchen appliance, for the wrong appliance has little long-term impact on their lives. Choosing the wrong plan for their life, however, could be fatal, people think, so they choose no plan at all. They fail to realize plans can always be changed. Others feel there is so much to plan that it will take forever. But remember this: for every hour you spend planning, you will actually save three to four hours of time. People think planning takes time; it does, but it also saves time. If you plan every day for the next day, you avoid the perplexing problem of what to do first. When you walk into your office with your written plan in front of you, you can spring into action immediately. People armed with a plan can accomplish more in several hours than any unfocused workaholic.

Another reason people tend to steer clear of planning the important things in life like financial security and career goals is that too many factors appear to be beyond their control. As the poet Robert Burns wrote, "The best laid schemes o' mice and men / Gang aft a-gley [often go astray]." While it is true there are some things outside our control, that does not obviate the vital need for a plan. A plan at least enables you to control those things that you can, in fact, control.

Planning does a lot more than just save time. It keeps you focused and makes it easier to get started, to take action. With some factors being outside your control, and with many other unanticipated events coming into the picture, you need something to keep you on your basic course. Sure, there may be roadblocks and detours, but a plan at least keeps you in the right general direction. A plan doesn't always tell you precisely how to get there, but it does serve as a guide or map that keeps you going, and it provides alternative routes, if necessary.

## Twelve Key Planning Concepts

### 1. Don't Abandon Ship

Before you develop your own plan, you must understand some basic planning concepts. One fundamental concept is sticking with the plan.

Most people abandon their plans at the first obstacle. They feel that since a problem has arisen, it proves the plan won't work. This is a big mistake. You will run into setbacks with any plan; they are unavoidable.

A fine example of this was the D day invasion in June 1944. The Allies, under the direction of General Dwight Eisenhower, had planned meticulously for the landings. However, the weather was not cooperating. A terrible storm threatened the Channel crossings. Many in the high command favored calling off the assault. But Eisenhower, refusing to give up the plan, gave the go-ahead. The rest is history.

All plans must be flexible, since in reality they are basically guidelines. Many a football team will modify its game plan at halftime. Great boxers feel out their opponents in the early rounds and adjust their plan in

95

order to counter their opponents. The key words are "modify" and "adjust." They will not totally abandon the plan, but without making modifications or adjustments, it is difficult to be victorious. Unforeseen events, such as turnovers or injuries, can wreak havoc on the original game plan. The reactions of the opposing team will also have an effect on the plan.

If Plan A doesn't work, try Plan B. If that fails, try Plan C, D, then E. You can always change the plan, but you must always have one. A failed plan must be viewed as only a temporary deviation from the overall plan. In the end, the plan, though changed and battle scarred, will be the thing that keeps you going.

Sticking to a plan also gives you a sense of control and raises your confidence. Following your plan requires discipline, and every successful exercise of discipline will make it easier to continue on a disciplined course. This, in turn, will greatly increase your self-confidence and your belief in your ability to follow through with the execution of your plan in the face of any adversity. You will have a feeling of great accomplishment as you complete each activity within the plan. You continue to develop momentum as you drive toward your goal.

## 2. Problem Solving

Never view a problem as an obstacle; see it as an opportunity. Failing to view roadblocks as opportunities will cause you to focus on the negative aspects of the situation. It is always difficult to formulate solutions if you are dwelling on the negative.

Learn to view problems as simply changes in external events. Sometimes these external events are beyond your control and thus force alterations in your plan. But they can also create enormous opportunities. Focusing on the new possibilities inherent in any problem can reveal hidden opportunities or possibilities. When the horrible Tylenol tampering cases arose, Johnson and Johnson, the makers of Tylenol, could have simply hidden from the problem. Instead, they embarked on a massive campaign to eliminate the problem and to communicate their feelings of responsibility to eradicate it. Instead of sitting by and watching the company destroyed, they actually strengthened bonds between the company and the consumer.

Never allow so-called problems to paralyze you. It is the paralysis, not the problem, that is to be most feared. When you are confronted with a problem, stop and think of the worst possible outcome. Resolve to accept the worst if it should befall you. Then do your level best to make sure it doesn't happen. Once you decide upon your course of purposeful action, begin executing it immediately. Taking action will reduce the anxiety. It is better to do something imperfectly than to do nothing.

We recently had a client consult us on a problem that had been hanging over her head for two years. The anguish on her face cried out for action. We told her exactly what she should do, and she gladly agreed to go along with our suggestion. That evening she called us back to say, "I don't know how I can ever repay you for all you've done for me." This was a rather strong statement considering the fact that we hadn't even begun to perform any legal services. Obviously our taking command of her problem and forcing her to finally make a decision took the weight of her problem off her shoulders. Regardless of the ultimate outcome, her true problem—paralysis and inaction—had already been overcome.

Whenever a so-called problem arises—and you'll know they are problems because those around you will label them as such—immediately think of all the possibilities created by this change in circumstance. A remarkable example occurred in the life of psychiatrist Viktor Frankl.

Doctor Frankl spent years in the concentration camps of Auschwitz and Dachau. Instead of giving up, he used his experiences in the concentration camps to study human behavior. His findings became the subject of his remarkable book, *Man's Search for Meaning.* His study of the concentration camp inmates led him to the discovery that the inmates who survived were generally those who had a plan for the attainment of goals. He sometimes referred to these plans as "unfinished business"—things that needed to get done, something to look forward to. It was easier to survive if life still had meaning. Frankl tells of one prisoner who had looked forward to a certain date he was convinced would be his day of liberation. Finally, the day came, but freedom did not. The next day he was dead; his goal had died. Man's hunger for meaning includes a longing for meaningful goals and plans. Frankl also discovered that although the Nazis had deprived him of most of man's basic freedoms, they could never rob him of the most precious freedom: the freedom to choose his attitudes. If the victim of a Nazi concentration camp can view this dilemma as an opportunity, surely we can do the same with our petty problems.

So-called problems shouldn't be shunned; they should be expected. If there are no problems with your plan, then there is a good chance that your goal is not ambitious enough. Furthermore, if your problems are minor or nonexistent, you will not be likely to attract the best people to help you. Talented, ambitious people are attracted to big problems.

Change is as unavoidable a part of life as death and taxes. Because change is inevitable, so are problems. Look forward to them. They will give you the opportunity to grow as you conquer them. Just change your attitude toward them. Each time you successfully adapt to the problems, your confidence will grow.

## 3. Don't Reinvent the Wheel

Another valuable concept in planning is that you do not have to invent something from scratch. Studies have shown that a mere 10 percent change or modification in the way things are currently going can make you rich. If you examine business success stories, you will see that they come mostly from those who merely added a slight change to an already existing concept. That small but significant change led to fortunes.

McDonald's didn't invent the fast-food business, but it certainly revolutionized it. In a relatively short time span, it grew to what is now an institution. Literally thousands of franchises made fortunes with this fast-food hamburger chain. However, White Castle was around with this concept long before McDonald's. But Raymond Kroc, the founder of McDonald's, improved upon the concept, setting a new industry standard. Conrad Hilton, founder of the Hilton Hotel empire, was not the first to conceive of a chain of hotels in various locations, yet his concept of cost-effective space utilization and service made him a fortune and led the way for a revolution in the hotel business.

Ralph Waldo Emerson said, "Our best ideas come from others." Human beings have been on this planet for eons. Time is too short to keep trying to start from the beginning. Adam and Eve had no choice, but you do. Before you begin your plan, read how others in your field have solved problems and created successful careers. If you can correspond with those who have succeeded in your chosen field, get to know them, and model yourself after them, you will be well on your way to success. Babe Ruth modeled his batting style after Shoeless Joe Jackson and then improved upon it. General Patton is said to have modeled himself after Alexander the Great. Human behavior is based upon role models. Most children initially model themselves after their parents. Truly wise people learn from the mistakes of others. Potentially wise people learn from their own mistakes. Fools never learn.

Plan to find mentors in your chosen field. Read about and study those people whose traits you would like to acquire. In fact, if you act like one of your mentors for a long enough time, you will inevitably become like him or her. In effect, having a mentor enables you to choose your own starring role. As you observe him, you will begin to see that he puts his pants on one leg at a time, just like everybody else. As you begin to realize that she also has her failings, it will dawn on you that if she can do it, so can you.

One of the first systems of written laws was developed by Hammurabi. Hammurabi had one piece of social legislation that would be more effective than all the social entitlement programs ever devised from the New Deal to the Great Society. Hammurabi made it mandatory for each person to be a mentor to another, to teach his skills, knowledge, and wisdom. This type of social engineering was certainly more effective than all the modern entitlement giveaway programs that wind up hindering the very people they are supposedly helping.

The Jewish philosopher Maimonides listed the various types of charity in the order of their priority. At the top, he listed "teaching others in the way of business." There's an old saying, "Give a man a fish, feed him for a day. Teach a man to fish and you feed him for a lifetime." We have gotten too far from this concept and now instead of teaching people how to "fish," we constantly throw them fish without exacting any effort

100

from their end. All this does is perpetuate their plight. Learn what you can from your mentor. Then begin to think creatively. How can you add to the evolution of the way things are done by your mentor and other successful individuals? Remember, a 10 percent improvement on the way someone else has done something can lead to a 1,000 percent improvement in your life.

## 4. Plan to Make What You Do Enjoyable

Confucius said that if you do what you enjoy, you'll never work a day in your life. In the last chapter we wrote that you must do what you enjoy or make what you do enjoyable. First, then, make your plan an enjoyable one to follow. Otherwise, you will never stick to it. How many times do people begin an exercise regimen? They psych themselves up and buy a health club membership, making the health club owners very happy. They follow the regimen for one or two months (if that long), and then abandon the routine. That is why the health spa chains have become so successful; they know from detailed statistical studies that they can sell many more memberships to their clubs than the clubs can actually hold. If all the people who enrolled in the clubs actually showed up, every fire law in the country would be violated. Fortunately (for safety's sake), so many people drop out of their exercise routines that the constant influx of new members never appreciably increases the crowd at the health club.

Why do so many people drop out of such routines? One of the major reasons is that people do not make their routines enjoyable. Exercise can be very boring and tedious. One may know he or she has to stick to a plan or a routine in order for it to have its desired effects. However, for most people that is just not enough incentive to keep going. Disciplined consistency is a

101

key to success in any endeavor, but it's difficult to be consistent if you don't enjoy what you're doing.

Before we started our own law practice, we thought the reason for our lack of success was that we had chosen the wrong field. As the cliché goes, "The grass is always greener on the other side of the fence." We reasoned that maybe it was time to switch to a field we would really enjoy. After exploring other fields, we realized that it is not necessarily the field you are in but how you play on it. We decided we would stick with law but try to make it enjoyable. The first step was to quit our jobs and start our own practice. This was necessary because our employers were not open-minded enough to react positively toward our innovations. They were our ceiling, and we wanted to raise the height of that ceiling. So we started our own law practice.

We had been singing, while in law school, for an orchestra in Great Neck, New York, and they offered us a "little room" in their suite in exchange for free legal services. Well, the price was right, but we hadn't realized just how little the room would be. It could accommodate only one tiny desk, and it had a large pipe running from the roof to the floor. Any time there was any wind on the roof, the pipe sounded as if Buddy Rich were beating out a drum tempo inside. We ordered a standard rotary phone with only one line. Did it matter? Of course not. Nobody called. You see, we didn't have any clients. We had failed to plan and therefore we were missing an essential for any law firm—clients. So much for small details. Though we borrowed a miniature typewriter from John's brother, we had another slight problem—we couldn't type and couldn't afford a secretary. Our index fingers became muscle-bound as we struggled over the course of an entire day to type a letter.

We call those days the bagel days. When we say bagels, we don't mean with cream cheese and lox. Each

102

day at noon we would take a half-mile aerobic walk to the local Great Neck bagel store and eat two dry twenty-five-cent bagels for our business "power lunch." Luxuries such as restaurant meals, shows, fancy clothes, jewelry, or cars were out of the question. Ronzoni spaghetti was the order of the day for supper. Luckily, complex carbohydrates are good for your health.

It was amid all this that we came across a book entitled *Think and Grow Rich,* by Napoleon Hill. Bob Unger's father-in-law, Jack Hollander, must be given credit at this point for having the book on his coffee table. We both read *Think and Grow Rich* several times and thought that it was a lot of hocus-pocus. However, one great advantage existed for us; we had absolutely nothing to lose. Though we could not agree with everything Hill wrote, he stressed writing down your goals and accurately detailing what you will give, or what service you will render, in return for the realization of your goals. Since at that time we had only a couple thousand dollars to our name, we decided that a modicum of financial security would be desirable as a five-year goal. In 1984, we wrote the following statement, hung it on our wall, and carried a copy with us:

It is January 26, 1989. I have accumulated one million dollars in total assets. In *return* (you must give in order to receive) for *earning* (anything worthwhile must be earned) the one million dollars, we will devote complete time and energy towards building our law practice. We will *constantly* and *consistently* (discipline and consistency equals success) become *involved* (you can't be successful sitting at home watching soap operas) in civic, political, and any other activities which will enable us to constantly meet and impress new

103

people. We will constantly give our business cards to these people. Having impressed them, whenever they or their acquaintances require legal assistance, they will come to us. (Notes in parentheses have been added for the purposes of this book.)

"Become involved" is exactly what we did. If three people congregated in an elevator, the Singing Lawyers were there handing out business cards. We handed out business cards as readily as meter maids hand out tickets. The phone began to ring. Pretty soon we had to get more phone lines and a bigger office, even a secretary. We also learned that becoming involved in this world returns rewards that cannot be measured by money alone. The satisfaction and self-fulfillment engendered by our activities can never be equaled in dollars and cents.

Our practice grew, but we were still one of thousands of law firms, and practicing law in a conventional way often seemed drudgery. One day we were asked to speak before the North Shore Real Estate Board in Queens, New York. While we were preparing our talk, it suddenly dawned on us that we might sing after we spoke. We had our reservations. Would it appear unprofessional? Would we be labeled "singers" instead of "lawyers"? Would other lawyers be scornful? These were all thoughts that popped up as we pondered the inception of the Singing Lawyers. Of course, there was the positive side. We knew that name recognition is a very important factor in selling yourself or anything else. No matter how great your product or how great your salesmanship, if you cannot get your foot in the door, it will be very difficult for you to get ahead. Even if you do get your foot in the door, your sales pitch will fall on deaf ears and a closed mind if you do not perk up the interest of the person or persons you are trying to sell yourself to. We decided the hook of the Singing Lawyers would be an attention grabber.

The North Shore Real Estate Board seemed the perfect place to try this technique. One of our major goals at the time was to establish a strong real estate practice, whereby we could spread our name throughout the local real estate industry. We spoke to others about our bold plan, and the vast majority thought we were crazy. This was a good sign. Many thought we would become the laughingstock of the real estate community and the legal profession simultaneously. But we were internally motivated, enough so to take these comments as a signal to go ahead. In fact, we thought that others thinking we were crazy might very well indicate that the Singing Lawyers was a workable concept. (After all, as the song goes, "They all laughed at Christopher Columbus / When he said the world was round.")

Another factor worked in favor of trying the Singing Lawyers. Since we didn't have any real estate practice, what could we possibly lose? Why should we worry about losing clients we didn't have in the first place? Why should we worry about what lawyers thought when few lawyers even knew we existed? As you can see, there is a great advantage in having little or nothing. There is only one place to go, and that is up. Those of you who are starting new in any field of endeavor should be happy. You are not bound by the shackles inherent in any established business. You are free to improvise and try new techniques. You are free to succeed. Those who are in established businesses should never lose their creativity, but very often they do and their businesses stagnate. Remember, the elephant is basically a prehistoric animal that has adapted through the centuries. Dinosaurs failed to adapt, and that is why we do not see them roaming around.

In addition, we understood the major rule in the sale of any personal service: people will not seek out your service or your product if they don't even know that it exists. We could be the most talented attorneys in the world, but if no one knew who we were, it would do us no good. *We* knew that we were good lawyers, but that fact was irrelevant without a client base. Some of the best runners in the world are running somewhere in the distant jungle, and some of the best singers are working in some sleazy clubs for a hundred dollars a night. Being the best at what you do is wonderful, but if no one knows about it, you will not be in demand.

If we had waited to build our practice gradually, we might have succeeded, but we didn't feel like waiting twenty years. In order to leap ahead of the crowd, we had to do something different. There were risks, but there were also great possibilities.

Leaping ahead of the crowd is often referred to as the leapfrog technique. When we went to law school, we were given the impression that in order to be a successful attorney, you had to first work for a law firm and put your nose to the grindstone. Then, maybe after seven or eight years, they would make you a partner. The problem with keeping your nose to the grindstone is that you don't see much besides the grindstone. If you are fortunate and happen to be on the "right track," you may fall into the right place at the right time in the right situation and become a partner. We had decided long ago we were not going this route because it was controlled by others who decided whether or not we should become partners. We decided to do a leapfrog routine, and by starting our own law practice we became instantaneous partners. Sure, we were kings without a kingdom, but nevertheless we thought we were kings.

The leapfrog technique applies in all aspects of life. In politics, for example, the standard way of doing things is

106

to join a local political club and start by licking stamps and handing out campaign literature. You keep your nose to the grindstone working for various candidates and one day you may actually have some influence in someone's campaign. From there, you may be put up by the organization as a candidate after you have moved up the ranks over a period of years. When Ronald Reagan ran for governor of California, he had never held political office in his life, and yet he became governor of the largest state in the country. This is a classic leapfrog move. When George Bush became ambassador to China, head of the CIA, and head of the Republican Party in the Watergate era, these jobs were regarded as well off the path to the presidency. Many said the vice presidency was also a dead end. The leapfrog technique breaks the mold of tradition; it circumvents others' rules about how you can become successful. Be a frog and plan to leap across the waters of mediocrity; overcome the staid preconceptions of how you are supposed to do things.

Another thing the Singing Lawyers had going for them is that they really did learn how to sing. Singing is not, as most people suppose, a purely natural gift reserved for those few people blessed with great voices. While some people differ in their musical ability, nearly anyone can sing. Great singers are made, not born.

Neither of us had natural voices. However, we both had a great desire and need to sing. Most people are closet and shower singers who sing into their hairbrush before the bathroom mirror when they think no one is watching. But most people will not do the tedious vocal exercises required for an hour every day, for five to ten years, to develop their voices. A woman once approached a concert pianist after the finale of his fabulous concert and gushed, "I would do anything to be able to play like you." The pianist calmly looked at her and said, "No, you wouldn't. Otherwise you *could* play like me."

While we were taking voice lessons, we had to endure the heckling of our peers and received little encouragement from anyone other than the best voice teacher in the world, Jim Lynn. One time, Bob sang with piano accompaniment in the casino of a summer bungalow colony in the Catskills. The owner pulled the plug on the microphone amplifier and said, "Come back when you learn how to sing." Despite the naysayers, we practiced and practiced and eventually began to develop professional voices. Bob's first professional job was a complete disaster and ended with the orchestra leader telling him, "You look like a scared rabbit up there. You'll never be a singer." This is not an uncommon experience for people in the entertainment business. Frank Sinatra was treated this way in many of the clubs he sang in as a young man in New Jersey. However, Sinatra, with his distinctive bravado, would answer, "You'll see, one day I'll be the biggest thing in this business." As they laughed, Sinatra became even more resolute. Everybody knows who turned out to be right.

Whether your voice is developed or not, it takes a lot of courage to sing in front of others. Most people fear singing or speaking in front of an audience. Somehow, we mustered enough courage to continue trying. It really didn't matter what the situation was, we sang. As the saying goes, "There are no matinees." Whether you are on stage in Carnegie Hall or in a subway car, if there is an audience, pretend it is the most important engagement of your life. That's what we did when we set out for our appearance before the North Shore Real Estate Board.

We both gave good talks. Then we told the audience we were going to entertain them with a song. There was surprised murmuring in the audience. We sang to the tune of the Julio Iglesias and Willie Nelson song "To All The Girls We've Loved Before." However, we changed the lyrics:

108

To all the deals you've lost before
That traveled in and out your door
You'll be glad we came along
We dedicate this song
To all the deals you've lost before

To all the deals you've seen fall through
Because somebody let them stew
Just call on us next time
We'll be there on the dime
For all the deals we'll save for you

The winds of change are always blowing
And every time there is delay
The winds of change continue blowing
And your deal will blow away

We knew these words would appeal to the brokers because they are often frustrated by attorneys who do not give priority to setting up contracts. It is a statistical fact that the longer you wait to bring an oral agreement to a written contract, the greater the chance the agreement will fall through. "Seller's second thoughts" and "buyer's remorse" are so common they have become clichés. The buyer begins to think he paid too much, and the seller begins to think he sold for too little. By singing the words as we did for the real estate brokers, we demonstrated not only our singing voices but our ability to empathize with them. The crowd loved it. The Singing Lawyers concept was born and so was our real estate practice. We now get referrals from almost every real estate broker in Queens and in the North Shore of Long Island, and we are the closing attorneys for several banks and lending institutions as well.

Sure, we still have to be good lawyers. No one would hire us just because we can sing. Our song provided a much-needed foot in the door.

109

Of far greater importance is the fact that singing has enabled us to make what we do enjoyable. Law is a difficult and often tedious profession. There is little glamour in it, in spite of what the television shows and sensational trials suggest. A recent poll disclosed that 60 percent of all lawyers dislike what they are doing. It is estimated that each year as many lawyers leave the profession because of emotional burnout as those who enter it. Singing has allowed us to take a difficult and tedious field and make it exciting and fun. And let's face it, the public's view of lawyers is not exactly favorable. Lawyers are seen as cold, insensitive, and money hungry. Once clients hear we are the Singing Lawyers, however, the entire atmosphere changes. In fact some people say we are the only lawyers who sing without being indicted first.

One day John went to a real estate closing at the offices of one of the bank's closing attorneys. Apparently, there had been a scheduling mix-up, and there were more closings scheduled than there were rooms available. When John arrived with his clients, he watched the secretary approach the head partner of the firm and give the name of John's scheduled closing. The lawyer gruffly responded, "Tell him it's too bad, we have no room. They will have to reschedule and come back another time." Just as he finished his sentence, however, the man looked up and saw John. His entire expression and attitude changed: "Oh, you didn't tell me it was the Singing Lawyer. Come right in, come right in, you know I used to sing too; I used to be in a quartet." When people learn that we are the Singing Lawyers, they often open up and trust us. They realize that lawyers are human beings also—at least some of them.

After we sang the national anthem for the Mets at Shea Stadium, Mets' announcer Gary Thorne, who also happens to be an attorney, recited a poem on WFAN radio that ended "We like lawyers that way [singing]."

The universal language of music has turned some hostile adversaries into gentlemen, some brooding judges into down-to-earth helpful jurists, and some suspicious clients into warm, trusting friends. Everyone seems to be impressed by two fellows who face the risk of singing in front of strangers.

Singing takes the harsh edge off the practice of law, making it enjoyable. Sure, we still have to do the detail work. We still have to go out continually and market and re-market. But singing has made it enjoyable, and that makes all the difference in the world.

In truth, we didn't invent the entire concept of the Singing Lawyers. Quite a few attorneys have made reputations as singers. But we don't know of another Singing Lawyers duo. And none to our knowledge have used their singing ability to motivate others and develop a law practice. In our case, by simply adding a 10 percent difference to the concept, we have been able to succeed. From our research on human achievement, we learned that scientists years ago discovered that music increases the frequency of one's brain waves; thus, singing (or music of any kind) makes learning easier. Think about how easily a child learns the alphabet when she learns to sing the alphabet song. Furthermore, repetition is the mother of all learning. People are more apt to repeat a message put to music. Music gives the Singing Lawyers that 10 percent difference, and makes people want to listen.

## 5. Do What You Do Best and Delegate the Rest

In following your plan, it is vital to focus your attention on your strengths. We all have strengths and weaknesses. If you work on your weaknesses, you can eventually become proficient in your weak areas. However, if you focus on and develop your strengths, you can become exceptional in a relatively short amount of time.

111

Too many people feel they must do everything and do it well. They become jacks-of-all-trades—and masters of none. While this is an admirable goal, it is not as effective as concentrating your efforts in a smaller area. At some point, you must delegate activities to others. Failure to delegate will leave you far behind in your plan and possibly transform you into a nervous wreck. While there is truth to the saying, "If you want it done right, do it yourself," if you do try to do everything yourself, you'll never have time to do the really essential things. There is never enough time to do everything. But there is always enough time to do the important things.

The ability to delegate is a key to success. It is a skill crucial to good management. Determine the activities that others can do as effectively or better than you. Delegate those activities and concentrate on tasks that you must do yourself, tasks that take advantage of your strengths.

## 6. Plan to Pay the Price

In order to execute your plan, you must be willing to exercise a great degree of self-discipline. Self-discipline means doing those things that must be done in order for your plan to succeed. You must do those things when you are supposed to do them. Here's the rub: you must do them even though you don't feel like doing them. You must do them even though there is something else you would rather be doing. You must do them even though they are hard to do. You must do them— period. Excuses like, "I don't have the time," "I'm too busy," or "I can't seem to get started" don't hold water. Make the time and take the time. Get busy doing what you must do and get started right now.

A fundamental truth in life is that you get nothing for nothing. When it is said that "the best things in life are free," the word "free" refers to monetary cost. Anything you get for nothing is worth precisely that: nothing. Even friendship and love require you to give something. Everything exacts a price. And the price must be paid. Failure to pay the price will not only result in failing to execute your plan and attain your goal; it will also mean you will still have to pay a price later on. Like inflation, the price goes up as time passes. If you don't pay the price now, you'll pay a higher price later. For example, if you can discipline yourself to save money while you are young, then you don't have to worry about being penurious and dependent when you are older.

Saving money requires discipline. Saving money means going without certain things for now. Surprisingly, however, the cost is not as great as you might think. The following chart was supplied to us by Tom Doumani and Joseph Townsell of Advanced Planning Concepts, Inc., of Orange, California; it shows just how little is required to ensure a secure financial future. If you can save about $59 per week beginning at age thirty until you are sixty-five years old, you can retire with an income of $60,000 per year, and over half a million dollars in savings. The table below shows how much you'll have to save each year until age sixty-five to generate various levels of retirement income:

|  | | Annual income at age sixty-five | | | |
|---|---|---|---|---|---|
|  | | $20,000 | $30,000 | $40,000 | $60,000 |
| Age at which savings plan begins | 30 | $1,022 | $1,340 | $2,044 | $3,066 |
|  | 35 | $1,552 | $2,332 | $3,109 | $4,665 |
|  | 40 | $2,409 | $3,614 | $4,818 | $7,227 |
|  | 45 | $3,849 | $5,773 | $7,697 | $11,546 |
| Total saved | | $176,126 | $264,190 | $352,253 | $528,379 |

If you are unwilling to pay this rather modest price and instead save nothing, your future is likely to be one of poverty and financial dependency. What a terrible price to pay!

Similarly, if you wish to remain healthy and live a disease-free, long life, you have to pay a price. You must not smoke, eat foods derived from animals, or drink excessively. In addition to refraining from the negative habits, you must also develop positive health habits. You must exercise every other day, get adequate sleep, and learn how to relax and deal with stress.

All beneficial and positive results require that you pay a price. Some people think that taking care of yourself in this fashion is too high a price to pay. But if you fail to pay the price now, look what can happen—cardiovascular disease, diabetes, cancer, or other degenerative diseases. The medical costs alone (not to mention the cost in loss of life and wages) is astronomical. However, if you decide to take care of yourself, the rewards are indeed great—a healthy, long life spent with your family, watching your great grandchildren grow up and have their families.

This rather simple formula works in every area in life. Some parents, for example, do not make time to spend with their children. In their rush to have what they want right now, they sacrifice the nurturing years with their children for higher-paying jobs that keep them away from home. Time and love are by far the most valuable things you can give your children. Temporarily you may have to forgo that new condominium you want to buy or that extra vacation. However, it is a relatively small price to pay for raising children who will fare better against drug pushers or those seeking to engage them in other activities injurious to their welfare.

With so many demands on our time relating to careers, it is hard for some parents to find time for their kids. Again, however, as the years go on, the price increases. At best, the children grow up indifferent toward their parents. Too often, however, neglected children become angry, self-destructive young adults who succumb to drugs, alcohol, or antisocial behavior.

Instead of thanking God for enabling them to participate in the wonders of creation, some parents look at their children as burdens. They will never know the true joys of life. If parents are willing to pay the price of listening to their children, spending time with them, and loving them, the results can be marvelous. Children then develop strong internal motivation and self-respect. They say "no" to drugs and all peer pressure. They respect and love their parents, and a rich and rewarding family life develops.

Sadly, though, America has become a quick-fix society that doesn't want to pay the price. We have actually been training people to think that they are entitled to something for nothing. We must all fight against this trend. People who get something for nothing really get nothing. They become dependent cripples who will never know the meaning and fulfillment one gets from discipline, sacrifice, and accomplishment.

## 7. Visualize the Plan

A very helpful technique in executing your plan is visualization. Learn to go through the actual sequence of planned activities in your mind. Picture yourself performing the particulars of the plan. See it, smell it, feel it, and hear it as if it is all really happening. If you can picture your plan in action, you will have a better grasp of its viability. For example, before we performed our closing song for the North Shore Real Estate Board, we visualized ourselves singing the song. We imagined the crowd and their reaction. Of course, we pictured a con-

115

fident delivery and an enthusiastic approval. With this exercise, we were able to establish a script for what was to occur. Then, with positive expectations, we went ahead and actually performed.

Another advantage to visualization is that it enables you to build up experiences. Even though the visualized experience is not actual, it is just as effective, if imagined in a sensory-rich way, as the experience gained by actually performing the task. By imagining the sights, sounds, and feelings of the situation, you will actually be propelled to continue your plan. In fact, when you have begun to exercise the plan, you may have a feeling of déjà vu.

Jack Nicklaus, perhaps the greatest golfer in history, said he always pictured himself completing his stroke perfectly in advance. He visualized the ball going where he wanted it to go. Likewise, picture yourself going where you want to go. Picture yourself performing all those steps that you need in order to carry out your plan and you will indeed get there.

## 8. Break the Plan into Its Component Parts

How do you eat an elephant? One piece at a time.

You cannot tackle a major goal by going after it all at once. An ancient Chinese proverb emphasizes that: "A journey of a thousand miles must begin with a single step."

We tend to forget that we must take many small steps to reach our big goal. In our enthusiasm and drive to reach our destination, we tend to throw ourselves headlong into our pursuit. The result can often be fatigue, disappointment, and frustration. This is precisely why a plan is needed. If we could accomplish our major goal in a day, we would not need a strategy. But that is not the way things work. In order to accomplish

116

anything, we must first set our goal. Then we must break it down into its component parts and achieve the mastery of each part as if it is an independent entity. Then we can go on to the next part. This procedure is continued until we have achieved each and every incremental step of the plan. For example, if your goal is to be a doctor, you would break down your plan into first becoming a college pre-med student, then achieving certain grades in pre-med courses, then achieving specific scores on the medical school aptitude tests, and so on. The beauty of a plan is that it allows you to look at each of the separate steps while at the same time looking at the whole of the plan.

When you look at a metal chain, you are able to see not only the entire chain itself but the individual links as well. The incremental steps of your plan can be likened to those links of the chain that are produced independently, yet when linked together form the entire chain. The third step is putting the component parts in sequence and prioritizing each component. The fourth step is estimating the time required to complete each component and assigning a target date for the accomplishment of each step. Finally, draw a flowchart that visually illustrates the plan as a whole and at the same time shows each of its component parts.

## 9. Establish Sequence

In order to bake a delicious cake, the baker must follow a recipe or plan. If the recipe, which is nothing more than a sequence of steps, is followed, the result or goal, a tasty cake, is assured. The real secret to any recipe, however, is not only the steps, but their sequence, too. Things must be done in their proper order. A lawyer must maintain a high grade-point average in college and then score high on the law school admission tests. He or she must then maintain a decent average in law school. Then the studying begins in order to prepare for a grueling two-day bar examination. The same sequence is necessary in sporting events such as football. If a pass receiver begins to run with the ball before he has actually caught it, he winds up running with his hands clutching the air. A great pass receiver always makes sure he has caught the ball before he begins to run with it. Failure to establish the proper sequence has caused great problems in all aspects of business and personal life.

When we started our own law practice, we were full of zeal, ready to work day and night for our clients. The problem was, of course, that we didn't have any clients. In our eagerness to get them, we tried to help everyone who might have any semblance of a legal difficulty. Often, someone would call with a very complex problem. We would spend days researching it. When we finally had gotten the answer and notified the client, the problem had either been resolved or the client informed us that it was no longer a real problem. He had just hypothesized a problem that might arise. We quickly realized that while our legal skills were sound, our sequence was way off. We learned that a client is not a client until he retains us. This simple and obvious realization saved us a lot of grief, money, and unnecessary labor. We learned not to invest our time on a legal problem until someone agreed to pay a fee for us to do legal work. It may seem simple, and it was—a simple matter of sequence.

Sequence is required in every business. Before a businessman can expand his venture, he must have the cash flow to generate monies needed for the increased overhead. Many businesses fail because they expand too quickly; their actions are out of sequence. Governments damage the economy when they spend money they haven't yet raised.

Even the act of singing requires the establishment of sequence. Our voice teacher, Jim Lynn, discovered this very early in his career and developed a technique that is second to none for building one's voice. Jim has been able to analyze vocal production and break it down into its component parts. He has also discovered the sequence of steps required to produce a rich-sounding voice. To develop your voice, you need only follow the sequence and exercise it on a daily basis, day after day. Admittedly, this is easier said than done.

The difference between a natural singer and others is that the natural singer came upon the right techniques as a child. He or she was applauded for the sounds he made, and the applause reinforced his technique. However, this is a hit-and-miss proposition. Most children do not find the right technique naturally and therefore they are not applauded. For the rest of their lives they think they cannot sing. They are deprived of one of life's greatest joys.

So, in many ways, discovering the right sequence is a master key to success. Once you find the correct sequence, all you need is the persistence and discipline to execute your plan. If you do not have the proper sequence, no amount of determination or willpower will ensure success. You will be an unguided missile. Guided missiles hit their target, whereas an unguided missile will hit sometimes and sometimes miss.

Finding the correct sequence ties in nicely with our earlier advice not to attempt to reinvent the wheel. Seek out those who have already succeeded in what you are trying to do. Then all you have to do is make some minor modifications and adapt their techniques to your abilities.

## 10. Develop Time Frames

Set deadlines for achieving each step of your plan. As we said in chapter two, these deadlines need not be poured in concrete. Planning is a trial-and-error process; we learn from our mistakes and successes along the way. Each time a phase of the plan goes well, take the time to analyze the various factors that contributed to the success of the plan. Then stick with those plans that have been successful. The same principle applies to setbacks. Each time you have a temporary failure, figure out exactly why things went bad and then make sure you do not make the same mistake twice. As the saying goes, "Fool me once, shame on you; fool me twice, shame on me." People for whom failure is a habit often repeat the same mistakes over and over again; they never muster the courage to take a good look at themselves to ascertain what they are doing to cause their own failures. In so doing, of course, they not only hinder themselves; they waste precious time.

Developing a time frame for your plan helps you to be ruthless with yourself in pursuing your goal and executing your plan. It spurs you to correct your mistakes and eliminate your weaknesses on a steady basis. Sometimes you will find that the closer you get to your goal, and the more you grow, the more your reality changes. If this occurs, it may become necessary for you to change your plan to fit this new reality—the new person you have grown to become. These types of changes are very positive, for the change in plan is necessitated by the fact that you have become a person who sets much higher horizons of accomplishments.

The old snowball theory comes into play again here. The accomplishment of each step in your plan creates greater momentum for following through with further plans. Visualizing your new horizons creates an emotional build-up that spurs you on to execute your plan. This in turn increases further emotional belief in your ability to achieve whatever it is you set your sights on. Take pleasure in each and every step of your plans and

120

savor every moment. After all, if we don't take pleasure in anything but our ultimate goal, we may never be happy.

Be happy with the small victories en route to your distant goals. The big victories only come around once in a while. If you don't take pleasure in the small advances along the way, you may not be able to exercise the discipline to wait for the ultimate goal, which may be twenty or thirty years away.

Despite the changes, alterations, or modifications that may occur in your goals and plans, you must keep setting time frames. If you don't, your plan will sputter and die like a car that has run out of gas. We recommend keeping your plan with you or within sight at all times. The flowchart we mentioned earlier is particularly helpful because it provides you with a visual blueprint from step one to your ultimate victory. With this flowchart in front of you, along with your detailed written goals, you will be constantly reminded of what needs to be done. Moreover, you can always check your progress against the flowchart. While doing this you can record each step that has been accomplished and go through your visual checklist to gauge your accomplishments. Constantly reviewing your past accomplishments will reinforce your determination and perseverance. If things go awry, you can backtrack to locate the point at which you went wrong. You will then be able to go back to the last successful step and begin again at that point with the knowledge of how you can make sure that the next step will be accomplished.

## 11. Execute the Plan

An old Chinese proverb says, "To know and not to do is still not to know." How true! You can read all the literature in your field and get expert guidelines from talented teachers; you can put together a detailed plan complete with flowcharts, time frames, and the proper sequence; in short, you can become a great professional student of success. But if you fail to act, you cannot hope to succeed. *Doing* is what separates winners from losers. Ideas and opinions, analysis and insight, education and knowledge, are fairly common. Only action determines value in the marketplace of life.

Without proper action, your plan, no matter how specific and well thought out, will fail. Without action you will never accomplish the steps outlined in your plan. You will be forever stuck at a phase in your flowchart. Success requires continued, consistent, and persistent action. Once you fail to act, your plan is null and void.

There are several techniques that will help you maintain the flow of action. It is most effective to do something each day that will move you toward your goal. People tend to procrastinate when they look too far into the future. In some cases, they have set their goal too high. In others, it is too far away. If you can't see your goal, you can't achieve it. Besides, viewing your plan in its entirety can be intimidating. The way to deal with this is to do something each day—anything, no matter how small, as long as it moves you toward the goal.

The point is to get started. *Do something.* This will create that momentum or positive inertia that will make the next step more natural. Action at each stage encourages further action. Action becomes a habit. Actions generate feelings. If you act as if you are confident, you will begin to feel confident. If you act as if you are in command of the situation, you will begin to feel in command of the situation. Once you get moving, you will find that any doubt you had whether you could fulfill a step in your plan was just plain silly. Your fears were just excuses to delay getting started. Most of the time doing something is not nearly as hard as it seems. Purposeful action has a way of making most so-called problems seem rather trivial. Inaction turns problems into crises.

Constantly letting problems evolve into crises is the result of a failure to plan. The habit is often referred to as brinkmanship. American politicians practice it daily. One glaring example lies in the criminal justice system. For decades lenient sentencing and plea bargaining have communicated the message that criminals can commit any brutal act with virtual impunity. Thus decent citizens peer out from behind bars while the criminals roam free. Now the politicians come out advocating strong plans to protect us. Had they simply enforced the law and executed stiff sentences for the last twenty-five years, they could have prevented the state of siege in our cities today.

## 12. Long-Term Planning

In our law practice, we have always opted for the long-term view. It calls for integrity, loyalty, commitment, and doing what is right as opposed to doing what is expedient. Businessmen who look only at the short term may do well, but only in the short term. The self-discipline to resist expediency and pay the price of success is a critical element in achieving it. Every act of discipline increases discipline; every act of expediency increases expediency. Successful people do what they have to do, when they have to do it, whether or not they want to do it.

For example, many people in business ask immediately, "What's in it for me?" This is the short-term view, and it is unlikely to engender long-term trust and business relationships. Once a local businessman, whom we thought was a friend, offered to introduce us to a very influential member of the government. We were grate-

123

ful to him for what seemed a desire to help us. But then he added the kicker. He would make the introduction only if we paid him a fee of ten thousand dollars. Of course we declined. This fellow made a fundamental error. By opting for the greedy short-term approach, he lost our friendship and trust, which were far more valuable than ten thousand dollars. Now that we know the kind of person he is, we will never associate with him again. Since we are in a strong position to recommend many people to his business, he has indeed lost a lot more than ten thousand dollars. Once we learn that a person's modus operandi is short-term, we drop him like a rock. After all, when you play in the mud, you are bound to get a bit dirty.

The American philosopher Ralph Waldo Emerson spoke of "the law of compensation." The law is a version of the biblical concept of "casting your bread upon the waters." It is much like the law of physics that teaches that each action must cause an equivalent reaction. Every time you help another to help himself, you help yourself. Unselfishness is ultimately the most self-serving characteristic you can ever have. Or as motivator Zig Ziglar puts it, "The best way to get what you want is to first help someone else to get what they want." What you put into your life in this world is what you get back—no more and no less. God plays no favorites. He does not discriminate. God is an equal opportunity employer.

We recently had a profitable experience with the law of compensation. A young fellow named John Ruggieri started an auto detailing business down the block from our law offices. The auto detailing business includes simonizing, pinstriping, and customizing top-of-the-line automobiles. One day we brought one of our cars to John Ruggieri to have it waxed and pinstriped. We were greatly impressed with his services, his hard work, and his insistence on doing the best possible job. His tremendous desire to help himself made us want to extend ourselves to help him. We introduced him to the success tapes and books we had used, and encouraged him to believe that he would be a success.

Several weeks later we received a phone call from a young man who had been seriously injured in an accident. He was unable to walk, so we had to drive to the South Bronx in the middle of the night to sign up the case. After we had met with the man, we asked how he had learned of our law firm. (Remember, always ascertain the reasons for every success that you have. This will enable you to plan future successes.) The young man reached into his pocket and pulled out a crumpled business card of ours. Printed on it was the barely legible name, "John Ruggieri." Get the message?

Of course, the long-term approach requires discipline and faith. But make no mistake; it works. Our entire law practice has blossomed because of it. Sure, it takes time, but most good things do.

This long-term approach should be followed in all areas of your life. In fact, many people do not take the long-term view because they have a short-term view of life. Recent scientific evidence suggests that our life span should be anywhere between 110 and 120 years of age. What hinders us in the attainment of such longevity is our mental attitude toward aging.

Dr. Kenneth Pelletier of the University of California in San Francisco determined that the chief factor in what determines our life span is our aging "set point." If we think, as society does, that age sixty begins old age, our body will begin to respond to that thinking. If, on the other hand, we view sixty-five as middle age (that is, half of our life span), our bodies will respond to the attitude. Ironically, the retirement age of sixty-five was set by Bismarck in prewar Germany, when life expectancy was only about fifty. Yet people still retire at age sixty-five today.

It was a one-hundred-year-old man who said, "If I knew I was going to live this long, I would have taken better care of myself." If you expect to live a long life, you won't take drugs. You'll eat right and exercise every other day. You will avoid the immediate gratification of life's quick fixes and instead reap a rich harvest of prosperity and long life. Plan to live for at least one hundred years. If you think and plan for the long term, you will probably live for the long term. Then we can all get together for a motivation seminar for centenarians who want to reach the age of 150.

# 4

# ATTITUDE, NOT APTITUDE, DETERMINES ALTITUDE

Why is it that we can have two people with equally underprivileged backgrounds yet only one of them manages to lead a successful, fulfilling life? Why is it that one of them focuses on what he is now, whereas the other focuses on what he will become?

Why is it that millions come to our shores from different nations, speaking different languages, yet succeed, while millions of native-born Americans flounder in poverty?

## Change Your Attitude and You'll Change Your Life

The difference lies in *attitude,* in the way people think. As we learned in the first chapter, you and only you are responsible for the way you think—for your attitude. It's your state of mind, the emotions you feel, your approach to life that dictates your circumstances. Unfortunately, most people allow their circumstances to dictate their attitude. If it's raining outside, they feel bad. If someone cuts them off in traffic, they get angry. In short, people react to their circumstances instead of creating them. Yet attitude is the one and only thing that is totally within your control. No matter how bad circumstances get, you and only you decide what your state of mind will be. Even if circumstances are dismal, a change to a positive outlook is the first step to changing those circumstances. If you want to change the external (circumstances), you must first change the internal (attitude).

Failure to understand this law has caused enormous misery and wasted billions of dollars. The failure of the social welfare program is a key example. Over the past thirty years, many social scientists have tried quite successfully to convince Americans that circumstances and environment cause people to flounder in poverty, take drugs, or commit violent criminal acts. Following this line of reasoning (or lack of reasoning), they insisted that all we had to do was change people's circumstances and all would be right with the world. And so ensued the Great Society, the war on poverty, food stamps, welfare payments, public housing, bilingual education, and billions spent on education. This country spends far more money on education than any other country on the face of the earth. If more money were indeed the answer to education, our kids would be the best educated in the world. Unfortunately, as our education expenditures continue to surge upward, our results continue to spiral downward. Instead of stressing excellence and the emulation of excellence in students, we hold the potential achievers back so that we won't make the others feel bad. In parochial schools, where teachers are paid a relative pittance, education is superior to that in our public schools. Once again the answer is found in attitude, developed by stressing discipline and character.

In the area of housing, we again follow the foolhardy path of concentrating on changing people's circumstances. We move people from ghettos to spanking-new high-rise apartment buildings. However, in a matter of years, the new high rises have become ghettos.

In every area, from public education to the employment marketplace, the so-called social engineers have tried to replace competition with a regimented mediocrity. This has furthered the socialistic goal of equal incompetence and equal deprivation for all. Isn't it ironic that while millions in the former Soviet satellites struggle to rise from the ruins of socialism and while thousands of Chinese are massacred in the streets of Beijing for turning toward the ways of the Western world, we in the West are becoming increasingly socialistic?

Isn't it ironic that the very people who express concern for minorities are instituting racist employment quotas which encourage minorities to believe the lie that they are inferior? Isn't it ironic that these professedly compassionate people push all the so-called entitlement programs that have made slaves out of people, robbing them of initiative and the incentive to extricate themselves from unfulfilled lives?

It should be obvious by now that changing one's circumstances is not the answer. The answer lies in changing attitudes—changing the way we think. If you change the way someone thinks, you don't have to change his circumstances; he'll change them on his own. He will rebuild or move from a ghetto; he'll educate and motivate his children; he'll open a business, create jobs, and expand the economy; he'll even expand the tax base.

The social engineers try to change the plight of the poor by altering their circumstances. Social entitlement programs give money, provide housing, and sometimes even give job training. But these programs are doomed to failure because the underlying attitudes of

129

people are not changed. The real challenge is to change their despairing acceptance of poverty. Public policy must encourage an attitude of self-sufficiency among the poor.

One shining example of such a policy is owed to Jack Kemp. While a member of Congress, Kemp sponsored a bill to privatize the Kenilworth Housing Project in Washington, D.C. The bill allowed the project to be sold to organizations of tenants. The tenants, led by Kimi Gray, formed a management corporation which has greatly improved the quality of life at Kenilworth. The management corporation also helps kids go to college and operates several businesses on the premises. Private ownership fosters self-esteem, whereas housing projects encourage dependence and degradation. In Kenilworth, free enterprise has changed the way people think, and thus their circumstances have improved.

If you attempt to change circumstances by altering the external, your success will be short-lived. However, if you change the way people think, circumstances can't help but improve; the improvement will be automatic and permanent. William James, the father of psychology in America, said, "The greatest discovery of my generation is that human beings can alter their lives by altering their attitudes of mind."

We can all be the masters of our fate. Everyone must take total responsibility for where he or she is in life. Many people who lead unproductive lives have difficulty coming to grips with this fact. People have a natural tendency to blame their failures on factors outside of themselves. This justifies (in their own minds) resentment, hatred, or even violence. Once again, isn't it ironic that the very people who purport to be concerned with the "underprivileged" encourage attitudes which doom them to a permanent state of being "underprivileged"? You see, if you have no control over

130

where you have gone, then it logically follows that you cannot control where you are going. The result of this way of thinking is to rob such people of hope—to bombard them with the attitude that they are doomed from the start, so why should they even begin to try?

Many others have joined us in acting on this philosophy, such as a Dominican-born man who grew up on the mean streets of New York City. Fernando Mateo, one of twenty-five children, dropped out of high school. (Unfortunately, for all too many kids, dropping out of school has become almost a means of self-defense. Fernando's school was inundated with drugs and drug dealers. He remembers sadly that even the school security guards were selling drugs.)

Fortunately, in his early teens Fernando worked in a furniture store, which taught him things he would not have learned in school. He learned how to deal effectively with customers, and he learned the art of the sale. The entrepreneur who owned the store was a master deal maker and master salesman. Fernando would watch and listen to his mentor at every opportunity. As he developed his selling skills, Fernando was moved from the stockroom to the sales floor, where he excelled beyond everyone's expectations.

Eventually, the time came to move on. With two thousand dollars borrowed from his father, who also cosigned the lease, Fernando opened a carpet store on the Lower East side.

In very much the same way we built our law practice, Fernando built his floor-covering business. He worked until midnight, and his early mornings were spent sliding business cards under apartment doors. He paid the required price and was ready, willing, and able to do whatever it took to reach high goals. He also developed superior knowledge of his product and provided superior customer service.

131

Today, Fernando Mateo's store, Carpet Fashions Floor Coverings, does approximately two million dollars in annual sales. There is one store at 111 Fourth Avenue and another one at 143 East 54th Street. However, success has not spoiled Fernando. He still works seven days a week, but would like to cut it down to only six so he can spend more time with his beautiful wife and two young children.

Despite his formidable schedule, Fernando still finds time to speak to prison inmates and high school kids. He spreads his philosophy of attainment everywhere he goes. For his efforts, he recently received The New York Chamber of Commerce's Small Business Award for Excellence in Business and Commitment to New York City. He says, "If you live in America, the land of opportunity, you have it made. Sure, there is some discrimination and other obstacles, but too many people use this as an excuse."

Fernando Mateo sums up his life and captures the essence of this chapter when he speaks of what he tells inner-city kids: "I tell them, it doesn't matter what color you are, it matters what your *attitude* is."

## Attitude Is a Choice

A positive attitude is something that everyone can *choose to have.* We saw an extreme example of this in chapter three, as Viktor Frankl chose and controlled his attitude in the concentration camps of Dachau and Auschwitz. The past decade has added another great hero to world history—Natan Sharansky. A man short in physical stature, he was a mental giant who refused to allow the subtle and non-subtle tortures of the Russian KGB to quash his spirit. When they literally stripped this Jewish refusenik naked, as part of their general method of undermining the prisoner's attitude, he made up his mind: "The KGB can never embarrass or humili-

132

ate me, only I can humiliate or embarrass myself." We recommend Sharansky's book, *Fear No Evil,* to all those who find themselves in their own personal prison.

## Positive Attitude, Not Wishful Thinking

Many people confuse a positive attitude with wishful thinking, a negative attitude with realistic thinking.

A positive thinker is not a wishful thinker. Positive thinkers do not operate on the basis of false assumptions. Positive thinkers have the courage to look reality in the face and see every defect that must be overcome or improved upon. They are able to see the dangers inherent in their path and thus can veer quickly in a new direction. They understand human nature and do not enter into personal or business relationships based on wishful thinking. They are not misled into believing that they will be able to change their prospective business or marital partner.

Americans have a well-intentioned but nevertheless dangerous tendency to view potential enemies, whether they be Communists or Nazis, from the perspective of wishful thinking. Our view of others is based on our cultural and moral standards. For example, when the Shah of Iran was deposed, most Americans felt that it was for reasons of liberation and freedom. In reality, the Shah was deposed because he was far too liberal for the fanatics who ousted him. When Hitler launched a maniacal quest for conquest and genocide, most people refused to believe the obvious. Again, we were assuming that others live by our moral and cultural standards. We paid dearly for that bit of wishful thinking.

Positive thinkers see reality even if it is, for the time being, not what they wish to see. They set a goal and develop a plan for the attainment of that goal. The goal is then pursued with a justifiably positive expectation of success.

133

## Attitude Creates Performance

Did you ever wonder why superior athletes can perform beyond all expectations on one day and like amateurs the next? Why does a Barry Bonds or a John Olerud bat .500 one week and .100 the next week? Surely it cannot be that they have lost their talent. Their physical condition is not a factor. Often the difference is attitude.

Sugar Ray Leonard was interviewed after a long absence from boxing, prior to his return-from-retirement bout against a previously unbeatable Marvin Hagler. In a pre-fight interview, Leonard was asked, "What will you do if you lose? Will you go back into retirement?" Leonard answered by saying that he is "incapable of considering defeat." Do we have to tell you who won? Mike Tyson and Mike Spinks were both interviewed prior to their championship bout. Spinks said, "I'll try my best." Tyson said, "I can't lose." Decide which fighter expressed the more definite attitude and you have named the winner. Winners believe they are destined to succeed and will succeed no matter what happens. Winners dwell on accomplishing goals. People who have not yet learned how to be winners dwell on lack and scarcity. The attitude of "I'll try," although admirable, often expresses an advance apology for defeat. Replace "I'll try" with "I will" and you have a new, positive attitude.

Think of the attitude of a young Cassius Clay repeatedly affirming "I am the greatest, I am the champion" in the face of the odds-on favorite, Sonny Liston. Think of Babe Ruth pointing to the part of the stands where he would hit a home run. Think of the last time you were under pressure to perform. Remember how fears of defeat began to seep into your attitude. Recall the physical manifestations of sweaty palms and increased heart rate. Maybe you blew the sale or struck out with men on base or sang off-key. In most cases it is attitude that makes the difference.

From one sale to another, a salesman's talents do not diminish. Long-term acquired ability remains consistent. However, it is much more difficult to consistently maintain a positive mental attitude. For example, visualize a sale that you feel pressured to make. Then imagine that you just had news that an unmarried relative you didn't even know existed had just left you ten million dollars. Out of a sense of responsibility you still make the sales call. However, your attitude has certainly been made more positive, and thus the sale is made with greater confidence. Now think what would have happened if news of the ten-million-dollar inheritance had been a lie. You still made the sales call. Once again, it would have been attitude that made the difference, even if the attitude was based on a falsehood. Later on in this chapter we will show you how by feeding yourself assumptions in the form of affirmations, you can change your attitude, whether or not those assumptions or affirmations are presently true.

## Simple But Difficult

Some may say, "That sounds simple, but it's not practical." The truth is, it is simple. If you are positive, you will achieve positive results. The difficulty lies not in the application of the rule, but in the environment. We live in a negative world. A study of newscasts made at the University of Washington found that nineteen out of twenty of the stories reported are negative. Another study found that 70 to 80 percent of what parents tell their children is negative. With all these negatives bombarding us, it is easy to feel "down." It requires effort to be positive.

135

Most people take on the attitude of others. If the people around them are down, they will also be down. If those around them are "up," so are they. The old saying is true: "Confidence is contagious and so is lack of confidence." Since so many people are negative, no wonder negativity abounds.

As we said in chapter two, human beings operate on the basis of inertia. Once you get in the habit of being positive, positive feelings flow naturally. Negative feelings, once started, also produce a flow of negative feelings. You must get started on the right path. Getting started is the key.

## Nine Essential Positive Attitudes

### 1. The Confident Attitude

Many self-confident achievers report that prior to their performance, they still experience nervous symptoms ranging from butterflies in the stomach to rapid respiration. However, the achievers have found techniques to overcome their jitters, whereas others are paralyzed by them.

The greatest roadblock to self-confidence is fear. The only way to defeat fear is to face it down—do what you fear to do. The old adage of getting right back on the horse after taking a fall illustrates the importance of facing your fears before they become entrenched. What we fear doing is never an insurmountable obstacle. It is the fear itself that paralyzes us.

If your greatest fear is public speaking, start small. Pick a course that ultimately will require you to give a talk before a class. Our knees used to knock together at the thought of facing an audience. It was only our great desire to perform before an audience that gave us the courage to walk on the stage when we had a bad case of the jitters.

136

A great aid in overcoming fear of speaking in public is thorough preparation. All experienced trial lawyers know that the most eloquent trial attorney can be bested by an adversary who has prepared his case in complete detail and already knows exactly what he is going to do and say. A speech consists of substance and delivery. If you walk onto the podium totally prepared with your substance, you have only to concentrate on effective delivery. If you are an inexperienced public speaker and have no idea what you are going to say, you will inevitably push the panic button.

The use of props, though certainly no substitute for inner assurance, can be a helpful aid in developing confidence. Anyone who has seen the classic Disney animated film *Dumbo* will remember that Dumbo's mouse friend convinced him that he could fly if he held a magic feather in his trunk. The feather inspired belief in Dumbo and, sure enough, his flying became the sensation of the circus.

You may not want to hold a feather in your nose but dressing like the person you want to be may help you to believe in yourself. Dressing like a lawyer won't pass your bar exam for you, but it will help you begin to *feel* like a lawyer.

If you are terribly self-conscious about your looks, there is nothing wrong with plastic surgery. It may help you, ever so slightly, feel better about yourself. Unfortunately, many people made beautiful by plastic surgery look in the mirror and don't see any change, because they have not changed the mental picture or self-image they carry around inside their heads. This is why it is so important to use props only as a stopgap measure to bolster your confidence while you work on the more important attitudinal changes. If you fail to work on your long-term self-image and cling only to props, you will experience what happened to Dumbo when the feather slipped out of his trunk and he was forced to fly on his own or crash.

137

## 2. Attitude of Risk Taking

The attitude of risk taking can best be described by the story of the young man who is asked by the school's bandleader if he can play a trumpet. The young man responds by showing up for the big game with his trumpet in hand. When the band begins to play, the bandleader is horrified to hear the clinker notes coming out of the young man's trumpet. The bandleader pulls him to the side and bawls him out, shouting, "Why didn't you tell me you didn't know how to play?" The young man replies, "How could I have known I couldn't play, if I never tried before?"

Many people never take risks, of course, because they fear failure. As we have learned, however, failure is often a very good sign because it is proof of the fact that you are at least trying. The trick, as we shall see, is to keep trying. Fortitude leads to victory, which in turn leads to greater positive expectations and thus a stronger positive attitude.

The meteoric success of Rush Limbaugh is a prime example of risk taking. Looking at the phenomenal success of his radio and television shows and his two best-selling books, it seems difficult to think of Rush Limbaugh as anything but a constant winner. Believe it or not, just a few years ago Rush was working for the Kansas City Royals baseball team as a glorified public relations gofer earning less than most menial laborers.

He had worked in radio off and on in various capacities, including spinning records, but had never really been given a chance to be himself. Rush came from a family of lawyers but had dropped out of college. Rush read voraciously, however, giving himself an education. This paid off when he landed a job as a radio talk show host in Sacramento, California. For the first time, Rush was able to be his own man on the radio and his show took off. A radio entrepreneur heard him on the air and offered Rush a business proposition. He offered Rush the chance to leave his hit show in Sacramento in exchange for taking a risk on the East Coast. Rush would broadcast for WABC Radio in New York City for one hour each day without pay. Following the New York City broadcast, Rush could then use the WABC studio to broadcast a show over approximately fifty stations throughout the country. If the national show succeeded, Rush would share in the profits. If the show failed, however, Rush would be out of luck. As they say in show business, the rest is history. Rush exemplifies the way of entrepreneurship and hard work, epitomizing the free enterprise system of America.

## 3. Attitude of Healthy Arrogance

Arrogance is defined as the *excessive* sense of one's own greatness. True arrogance can be a most distasteful trait. But many people confuse positive attitude and faith with arrogance. In other words, one who refuses to go along with the crowd and stands up for his own beliefs is often unjustly accused of being arrogant. If this is arrogance, then we will refer to it as healthy arrogance, and, believe us, you need plenty of it. Ignore the oddsmakers and the experts because *they are not you*. Ignore all those who have tried and failed to do what you are now trying to do because they are not you. Experts and oddsmakers make their predictions based on past experiences. Surely the past holds many lessons for us, but one can never be sure of future potential. The fact that another person failed does not mean that you will fail. The fact that one technique did not work for another does not mean that the same technique will not work for you.

Many people seek advice from the "expert" hosts of radio call-in shows. Bob called in six years ago asking advice on whether to go ahead with the purchase of his first home. When the famous radio financial advisor learned how little our law practice was producing, he said "Let me be your Dutch uncle; do not buy this house!" As it turned out, the practice grew in leaps and bounds, and the house payments could easily have been made. An advisor you speak with for the first time advises you on the basis of what you tell him and on the basis of his knowledge of the field. The key missing ingredient is that *he doesn't know you.* You may be the exception to the rule. Acquiring a positive attitude will immediately make you an exception to the general negativity that exists in our society today. If you can become an exception to the general rule of negativity, then you can challenge most other rules as well.

Think in terms of possibilities. Respond to the rules set down for you by others with healthy arrogance: "Why not?" Believe that you can find the solution to any problem. Believe that there is a way to accomplish any goal. Remember, *they don't know you, but you do!*

## 4. The Can-Do Attitude

"Can-do" people are people who make things happen. They don't let ideas die on the vine. They write down their ideas and start immediately to make those ideas a reality. Their attitude is always positive because they are always working on something. Therefore, they always have something to look forward to. Having a can-do attitude is surely the antidote for depression. So if you're depressed, make something happen; create something, begin something. This will keep your expectation level up and thus keep your chin up. The actions don't have to be monumental. Do something every day that takes you just a little bit closer to your goal.

Everyone can do things. It is wrong to say you can't. Even if you may not know *how* to do something, you can still do it. The word *can't* is probably the most foul of the four-letter words. Strike it from your vocabulary. When someone tells you, "You can't do it," tell them, "You're right, *you* can't do it." Unfortunately, others will attempt to project their own self-created limits onto you. Don't let them. Only you can decide what your limits are. Maybe you'll even decide that you have no limits.

Immunize yourself from the doldrums by constantly refilling yourself with a positive attitude. Make sure the news is not the first thing you listen to in the morning. Turn on motivational tapes during breakfast or on your way to work. You'll find that your batteries remain charged with can-do energy throughout the day.

## 5. Attitude of Service

Truly successful achievers do not look at money as the purpose of their work. Money is simply something that comes with the territory. It is the aftermath or result of their having rendered service. The more service they give, the wealthier they become. Their wealth is not only evidenced by their bank accounts but by the richness of their lives. Remember one thing: nobody is buried with pockets. However, the service that you render and the thoughts that you nurture to life will remain when you are long gone.

When the Bible speaks of casting your bread upon the waters, it is referring to the everlasting principle that the more you put into life, the more you get out of it. Giving to and helping others is therefore the most selfish act that you can perform. As Maimonides said,

141

"Help others in the way of business and you shall be truly charitable." Help others to help themselves and you will be helped to an even greater degree.

Unfortunately, in the past few decades our society has gotten away from the attitude of service. We have become a quick-fix society that stresses the idea of making a killing. We play lotteries, horses, casinos, and penny stocks. Feeling good is almighty and sacrifice is scorned. Workers demand fewer hours and more pay. In other words, work less and make more. This goes against all laws of success. If you want to make more, you've got to give more, not less. In the short run, fewer hours and more pay will place a few extra dollars in your pocket. But in the long run the policy may destroy this society, the society that supplies jobs to workers.

We have gotten away from the work ethic that built this great nation, and we have reneged on our commitment to excellence. We have reneged in our schools and in the workplace. Maybe those old-fashioned values were developed for a good reason—because they work.

Instead of listening to those who exploit anti-Oriental bias, our leaders should be stressing a back-to-basics approach. We know the Asians are generally successful. The 1980 census revealed that the median family income of Asian-Americans was $23,000 compared to $19,000 for native-born Americans. Only the newly arriving refugees of Vietnam, Laos, and Cambodia were below the national average in 1980. By 1986, they too had overtaken it. In 1980, 75 percent of Asian-Americans were high school graduates, compared to 66 percent for all Americans. Asian-Americans also possessed twice as many degrees of higher learning; they had superior scores on the 1989 Scholastic Achievement Test (SAT). The Asians are no smarter than anyone else. The United States has won more than ten times the number of Nobel Prizes as all Asian nations combined. No racial group is innately more intelligent than another. The difference lies in the values of discipline, excellence, family, plain old-fashioned hard work, and *service*.

A revealing story was reported by officers on the carrier *Midway* who stopped to pick up half-starved Indo-Chinese boat people from their leaky, overcrowded rafts. As one of the refugees hobbled aboard, his body ravaged by dehydration, he faintly waved his hand and whispered to the sailors, "Hello American sailor, hello freedom man." Yes, freedom man: that's what America has been to the world. Perhaps those people fleeing from communist tyrants have a greater appreciation for freedom in America. Perhaps native-born Americans take their freedom too much for granted.

## 6. Attitude of Belief

Belief is the magic that breathes life into your goals. Belief provides the fuel for the perseverance you need to allow the laws of success enough time to work.

We know that one acts in accordance with what one believes to be true about oneself. If a salesman believes that he is a $30,000-a-year man, that is exactly what he will be. The same applies if he believes he's a $100,000-a-year salesperson. You will find that if a $30,000-a-year salesman who believes he is limited to that figure earns $10,000 in one month, his sales will tend to fall off until his monthly average commission drops back down to the $30,000-a-year level. Belief is a key factor in the makeup of any great salesman. Any salesman who can sell himself a product will have little or no trouble selling to his customers.

We know what belief does for our health. It can keep us healthy and vibrant or turn us into hypochondriacs.

143

Belief is contagious. It will cause others who are moved by your belief to become your allies. Mahatma Gandhi changed the beliefs of his nation and the entire British Empire with his belief.

We have known many people who were commonly perceived as "having nothing going for them." These people seemed to lack any marketable skills and certainly didn't have any educational degrees. One person was a guitar player barely making a living. The one thing he did have, as we look back at him, was a belief that he would be a success. We remember him persistently expressing this belief, and we remember ourselves trying to hide our disbelief. He started a club date orchestra and became a millionaire in his thirties.

We would be remiss in any discussion of beliefs to omit mention of belief in God. The order and consistency in the laws of this world inescapably support the existence of a Creator. All one has to do is act consistently with these immutable laws and his life will take on great meaning and fulfillment. Unfortunately, few people act in this way and thus we have so many trouble spots throughout the world and so many troubled individuals. People with belief are strengthened in a way that cannot be explained solely in terms of the human mind and body. Belief or faith is the bridge between the powers of humanity and the ability to rely upon the powers of God.

## 7. Attitude of Self-esteem

The attitude of holding yourself in high esteem stems from the acknowledgment that you are in command. It is a "take-control" attitude that does not recognize excuses and alibis. It is the attitude of "I'm in the driver's seat." The principles discussed in this book lead to self-esteem because the knowledge and execution of these principles lead to positive results; those results, in turn, further increase self-esteem. This creates a cycle of success.

Act in a manner consistent with your underlying moral and ethical principles as discussed in chapter two. In other words, act with integrity. Each time you act against your principles, you lose a degree of self-respect. You may gain in the short run, but you'll lose in the long run. For example, although cheating a customer will fatten your daily take, the damage it will cause to your self-respect will result in further losses.

Learn how to accept compliments. You deserve them. People with self-respect swallow and store compliments as a cactus plant stores water. Replace the uncomfortable denial of a compliment with a simple "Thank you very much; I appreciate the compliment."

Negative emotions are caused by our choosing to react in a negative way. Fend off these negative emotions with the previously discussed affirmations. Replace negative reaction with the words "Only I am responsible." These words will remind you that, as Viktor Frankl said, "You have the power to choose and control your attitude."

Rid yourself of the destructive negative emotions of jealousy. Today's political and social climate fosters resentment against achievement and jealousy toward those of greater material wealth. The 1988 Dukakis presidential campaign slogan of "I'm on your side" has the dubious distinction of further encouraging antipathy toward those who have achieved, and the 1992 Clinton campaign practically characterized achievement as a crime. This kind of resentful thinking will preclude the resenters from ever becoming achievers. It is also very damaging to self-esteem, because jealousy is an indication that you believe you can never achieve as much as those you envy.

145

Groucho Marx once joked, "I wouldn't want to belong to a country club that accepted me as a member." Unfortunately, people with low self-esteem actually do feel this way.

Don't fall into the trap of bitterness and envy. Align yourself with talented people. Become a bird of the same feather and flock together with achievers. They are your future allies. We all need allies. No one accomplishes much alone. Associating with people of high caliber will necessarily raise your level of self-esteem. Remember, you will subtly and overtly communicate to others the way you feel about yourself. The way you feel about yourself will be consistent with the way you are viewed by others.

## 8. The Silver-Lining Attitude

We recently did a success sermon along with some gospel singing for Deacon Ed Eason and the Westbury Gospel Tabernacle Church in Westbury, New York. The Art of Living Voices Choir, led by the superb Alfred Miller, opened with an old gospel song which goes, "In every dark cloud there's a silver lining, / Just look and you'll find it if you keep pressing on." Whether you realize it or not, the seeds of future victories can be found in every defeat; the seeds of rebirth exist in every tragedy. Successful people look for the bright spot in the darkest of circumstances. How many times in your life have you felt that a particular problem would be insurmountable? Now, in retrospect, you can see that it wasn't the end of the world. You survived. If Viktor Frankl and Natan Sharansky can find positive results from their experiences with the Nazis and Communists, then so can we with regard to our problems.

W. Mitchell epitomizes the silver-lining attitude. When Mitchell was twenty-eight years old, a motorcycle accident left him scorched over 65 percent of his body and burned off his face. His fingers were mangled and his bones fractured, but his spirit was not broken. Several years later he started a business and become a millionaire. Mitchell was so successful that he purchased a private airplane that carried him into new dark clouds. The plane crashed, and he was paralyzed from the waist down. But he still couldn't be kept down. As Mitchell tells it, "Before, there were ten thousand things I could do, now there are nine thousand. I could dwell on what I lost but I prefer to focus on the nine thousand things left."

Mitchell ran for Congress in 1984 using the slogan, "I'm not just another pretty face." Though he lost, he was not discouraged. He is much sought after as a public speaker. We recently had the pleasure of meeting him at the National Speakers Association Convention. We learned that his major accomplishments, including his marriage, came after his accident.

Captain Gerald Coffee was not confined to a wheelchair, but he was confined to a Vietnamese prison for a number of years. Captain Coffee kept a healthy perspective by reminding himself that the squalid conditions in prison were no worse than the living conditions of the Vietnamese people outside the prison walls. The communists could never break him or the men he held together with the glue of faith in God and faith in his country.

John Walsh, host of Fox Television's *America's Most Wanted,* has devoted the remainder of his life to the prevention of child kidnapping and abuse. His young son Adam was kidnapped and murdered; his assailants were never caught. John's show has led to the apprehension of scores of heinous criminals. John Walsh has not only survived the most horrible fate that can befall a parent, he has contributed by saving the lives of future victims. What greater legacy could any man ever leave his children?

Victoria Schneps, publisher of the *Courier* newspaper in Queens, New York, lost her daughter Lara recently. Lara was born mentally retarded and spent her early years in the Willowbrook institution. When her parents observed the horrendous conditions there, they took her back to care for her at home. Victoria and her husband Murray immediately notified Geraldo Rivera and other news reporters and together they exposed the outrageous neglect that was occurring at Willowbrook. Lara eventually died at home of natural causes. Because of their personal tragedy, Victoria and Murray worked to found and develop WORC (Working Organization for Retarded Children), which works to deinstitutionalize the mentally retarded by placing them in supervised private group homes that are purchased by the organization. Once again, a terrible loss serves as impetus for improving the lives of others.

Compared to the loss of a child, aren't our minor defeats inconsequential? If something positive can grow from tragedy, then surely something positive can be gleaned from the relatively minor mishaps that we experience every day. People fired from jobs without warning are forced to enter a new field that leads to a fortune. As it turns out, the boss they thought had ruined them turns out to have done them the greatest of favors. A blind Stevie Wonder, Ray Charles, or Ronnie Milsap leaves an indelible mark on the music industry. The human mind compensates for what the body is denied by releasing previously untapped power.

Learn from your defeats and disappointments and use those lessons to prepare yourself for future victories. Ralph Waldo Emerson hit the nail on the head when he said, "A healthy personality is determined by the degree to which you find something positive in every situation." Just look and you'll find it, if you keep pressing on.

148

## 9. The Don't-Take-Yourself-Too-Seriously Attitude

We think it appropriate to end our discussion of attitude with a caveat: take this material and yourself seriously, but never too seriously; put it in the proper perspective. We often tend to exaggerate our own importance. In reality, our lives are just little grains in the sands of time. Have fun doing what you're doing. Some workaholics feel guilty if they have fun. The fact of the matter is that you will always perform better if you are doing something you enjoy.

Don't magnify your problems. This applies doubly to money problems and to problems with material objects. Anything material can eventually be replaced.

We are all consumed with the problems of business, mortgage payments, finance, taxes, taxes, and taxes. These petty problems will dominate our life, if we let them, but they vanish when, God forbid, we face a real problem such as the bad health of a loved one. The old saying, "If you've got your health, you have everything," rings true here. If you have a healthy family, take time out to thank God and count your blessings.

Give thanks for being able to live in this great country. In 1989, television news brought into our homes a picture of a young unarmed man, on the streets of Beijing, placing his body in the path of a military tank. We watched the Chinese students erect their own version of the Statue of Liberty and hold it upright in the face of the Communist Chinese government. Ironically, at the same time an American (we use this term loosely) made headlines for burning the American flag as a symbol of his desire to bring about, in this country, the very same system that massacred three thousand students under direct orders of the Communist Chinese government.

149

We recently had a phone call from a client who was in the middle of a divorce proceeding. It was New Year's Eve and we ended our discussion by saying to the client, "Have a happy New Year." His response was a self-pitying "What do I have to be happy about?" Our advice to him (and anyone else out there who may be wallowing in self-pity) was to visit St. Mary's in Bayside, Queens, where he'd see ailing children. Or visit Danny Thomas's St. Jude's Hospital in Memphis, Tennessee, where children lie in bed with bodies ravaged by cancer and radiation therapy. Many of them are smiling and laughing with hope. You owe it to them, and to yourself, to show at least half as much character as they demonstrate every precious day of life. The parents of these children demonstrate a depth of spirit, devotion, and resolution that casts a giant shadow over our petty travails.

There's an old story about a group of people who form a circle. Each tosses his problems into the circle for all to see so they will have the opportunity to take on the problems of others while getting rid of their own. But, when the people see the problems of the others, they quickly dive into the circle to retrieve their own. Count your blessings; they are all around you.

# 5

# SEVENTEEN WAYS TO DEVELOP A POSITIVE MENTAL ATTITUDE

In this chapter we describe some powerful techniques to ensure a positive
mental attitude. These techniques are
simple. But do not be deceived by their
simplicity. They are extremely effective.

## The Old View and the New

For many years, psychologists and
psychiatrists felt that we could only
bring about change in people after
many years of intensive therapy.
Human beings are complex. Therefore,
it was assumed, we require complex solutions. This thinking, by the way, has
unfortunately carried over into the area
of social and political reform. We are
told that the problems are multifaceted
and therefore we must find equally
complex and expensive solutions. This
approach has not worked because it
does not square with reality.

Slowly, over the years, mental health
professionals have come to the eye-
opening revelation that complex solutions do not solve complex problems;

simple solutions do. In their book *Mind Power,* Bernie Zilbergeld and Arnold A. Lazarus, both clinical psychologists, make the point: "Many other consultants, therapists and physicians have come to the same conclusion. We have to admit that sometimes we're even a bit embarrassed about these techniques (visualization, self-talk, etc.). After all, mental training is so simple and easy, when compared to most other therapeutic methods, that it seems incomprehensible that it works as well. Something this effective should be harder, we sometimes think."

God did create a highly sophisticated creature when he made human beings. But he was very careful in his design. While he created an extremely intricate mechanism, he made the owners' manual simple so that we could use it. How many personal computers lie idle because the software program manual is complicated? KISS (keep it simple, stupid) has become the rallying cry in the business world. If it's not simple, you won't use it.

Think of automobiles. Most car problems can be solved with a minor adjustment. Once a loose bolt is tightened, this complex machine runs smoothly. Just because a car breaks down doesn't mean you need a complete engine overhaul.

Some may think it embarrassing to believe that their problems can have simple solutions. One might think, "Gee, if it's so easy, why didn't I think of that?" Imagine how a mental health professional feels after spending many years studying human behavior and traditional treatment modalities only to realize that simple visualization or self-talk can cure the problem quickly and effectively.

The simple approach also takes away the excuses that one conjures up in order to avoid change. Formerly a person could say, "I'd like to change, but I don't have the money or time to spend; I'd like to change, but it requires too much effort; I'd like to change, but there's no proof that any method really works." These techniques force us to face the fact central to this book: we have the power and the responsibility to improve our lives. If we change the internal, the external will also change.

All the excuses are now dismissed. Exhaustive studies, and (more importantly) real-life experiences have shown that these techniques are very effective.

## Techniques That Work

### 1. Expect Greatness

We know that we can choose our attitude. Let's look into how we go about doing so. Attitude is very much based on how we view our lives and our world. If we expect success, it naturally follows that we will have a positive attitude. It also follows that if we have been trained to expect failure and despair, we will think in a way that leads to exactly that. However, there is hope. Great minds in this country have discovered that expectations and attitude can be manufactured. In other words, we can create our own state of mind or thought. The great acting teacher Konstantin Stanislavsky knew this when he taught the "method" techniques of acting. Dr. Karl Pribram of Stanford University discovered that people who visualize themselves already in the possession of those goals they desire develop an extremely positive attitude.

Recently an experiment was tried in a public school in California. Teachers were told that because their teaching was so superb, they would be given the brightest and best students for the year. At the end of the school term, the teachers were not surprised by their students' superior performance. However, they were quite surprised when it was revealed to them that they had been tricked.

153

They had not been given the superior students they were told they were getting; they had been given average students. So why the superior results? Although much more research must be done, experiments like this one indicate that teachers subtly communicate their expectations about the students' performance to the students. The teacher's expectations, transferred to the students, control the attitude of the students and thus their performance. People generally rise to the level expected of them. John Steinbeck declared, "It is the nature of man to rise to greatness if greatness is expected of him." Expect greatness of yourself and others and you will be amazed at the way greatness will come.

## 2. Act "As If"

Attitude is not only the way we think of ourselves; it is also the way we feel. Feeling and thinking can never be completely divorced from each other. We are whole human beings with emotion and thought intricately intertwined. Traditionally it has been assumed that we act *as a result of* what we think and feel. However, it has been discovered that we can intentionally *act* our way into thinking and feeling anything we wish.

Actions are perceived by our subconscious mind as commands, and we respond to those commands by feeling what is consistent with the actions. In other words, intentional actions generate feelings consistent with those actions. For example, psychologists have been able to manufacture depression in ordinarily happy people by simply having those people take on the posture, movements, and breathing patterns of depressed people. The same principle applies to making yourself feel happy. This is the principle of acting "as if." Acting as if you are happy will help you actually

154

feel happy. Acting as if you are extremely interested in a lecture that you have been unable to follow will help you pay attention to that lecture. The same applies to acting as if you are confident or acting as if you believe in yourself.

As a matter of fact, guilty people can outwit a lie detector machine by using this technique. They simply act as if they believe what they say, and after awhile they are able to manufacture a false belief that what they are saying is true. A more extreme example of this is found in psychopathic liars. Hitler hypnotized a nation by persistently telling big lies as if he himself believed them. As we shall see when we discuss the law of suggestion, statements repeated to the subconscious mind, whether true or false, will eventually be accepted as true.

Actors who use the method technique become so engrossed in their role that after a while they begin to actually think and feel like the person they are playing. If this occurs for the several months that an actor plays a role, just imagine how you can program yourself if you work on it over the course of your life.

Emulate and act like the successful mentor we spoke of in chapter three, and you will begin to think and feel like him or her. This concept of creating attitude is nothing new. William Shakespeare said, "Assume a virtue if you have it not."

You can choose positive emotions by choosing activities that bring on those emotions—associating with positive-thinking friends, going to church or synagogue, reading motivational books, listening to motivational tapes. You can choose positive language. The next time someone greets you with the usual "How are you?" don't respond with the usual "Fine" or "OK." No matter how you feel, respond with "I'm great." Who knows, it just might help you to feel great.

155

### 3. Birds of a Feather Flock Together

Without question, we react to our surroundings. If we want to maintain a positive mental attitude, we must learn to control our environment. Professor Mc-Clellan of Harvard University found that no matter how much attitude training a person received, his attitude, to a large degree, was determined by the people with whom he associated. Peer pressure is a key element in determining mental state.

A young researcher was trying to find the secret of success. He sought out an extremely successful businessman. After following this businessman for years, the researcher finally was able to get an interview. He asked him what the key to success was. The businessman, without hesitation, said, "Stay away from the losers."

One of the reasons so many people are on drugs today is peer pressure. "Show me your friends and I'll tell you what you are" is a sound maxim. Befriend positive people and you will be positive. Befriend negative people and you will be negative. It's easier to follow the crowd, most of whom are "down." It requires effort to avoid the negative pressures of the peer group. It takes effort to go against the grain and be positive. However, the effort is well worth it. Once you begin, you can never go back to the old way of thinking.

### 4. Get Off the Fence

A major factor in establishing a confident attitude relates to our discussion of goals in chapter two. Confident people know what they want. They take a stand. They believe in what they are doing.

Don't spend your life sitting on the fence. Marry a set of ideals and principles worth believing in and fighting for. This book may anger some people due to the

156

strong principles that we espouse. Nobody who takes a stand will please everyone. On the other hand, who would want to read something so bland that it catered to the opinions of everyone? Stand against the tide, and one day you may become the tide. Jesus was crucified; Columbus was laughed at for believing the world was round; Marconi was temporarily committed for believing he could invent the wireless; Galileo was threatened with death; Joan of Arc was burned at the stake for her beliefs. People sneered when men spoke of spacecrafts to the moon. Many scoffed at Reagan's Strategic Defense Initiative (SDI), yet many others—from Russian generals to former British prime minister Margaret Thatcher—have since identified the pursuit of the "Star Wars" concept as a contributing factor in the collapse of the Soviet Union. Having strong beliefs predisposes you to being confident because you know where you want to go and therefore expect to get there.

## 5. Capitalize on Your Own Uniqueness

Why is everyone so concerned with blending in with the crowd? "Fitting in" is often detrimental, especially when the crowd is taking drugs or engaging in other unproductive and destructive activities. Be a shepherd, not a sheep. Sheep wind up as sheepskin. If you're just like everyone else, you're just average. Why not seek excellence? Why not become the best that you can become? No test ever devised can accurately predict potential. Therefore, you have no idea how great you can possibly be. Why not find out?

If you've got red hair, rejoice in the fact that you will naturally stand out from the crowd. If you are unusually short, work on developing the talents that you have and you will stand ten feet tall. The differences that most people fear are often the characteris-

157

tics that make people successful. Where would Jimmy Durante be without his big schnozzola? How many points would Wilt Chamberlain have scored if he had been of average height? How many races would jockey Willie Shoemaker have won? Helen Keller's birth defects forced her to fully utilize those senses that remained.

All of us have gifts we can contribute to the world. We are each as unique as our fingerprints, and no two fingerprints in the world are the same. Take pride in being different.

## 6. Focus on the Wins and Turn Lemons into Lemonade

Another essential technique for gaining a confident attitude is to constantly run, in your mind, instant replays of your past successes. Forget about your failures. Those who constantly replay their failures wind up repeating those episodes for the rest of their lives. Those who dwell on past successes tend to duplicate those successes. This does not mean that one should rest on one's laurels. Laws of physics tell us that we can coast in only one direction, and that is downhill.

Although it is wise to forget our failures, remembering the lessons of the past and then using them constructively is important because history tends to repeat itself. Try maintaining a diary or scrapbook of past achievements. Whenever your momentum is temporarily slowed by fear or setback, go to the scrapbook and review pictures of your success or reread a success diary. Modern technology has brought us the video age. Videotape your presentations and review your successful ones. We always advise politicians to constantly review their most effective speeches in order to prepare for future speeches and debates.

If you don't have a video handy, then review your past successes in your mind's eye through the sensory techniques of visualization and sensory memory. At the same time, try to rekindle the emotions you felt at that time. Recall what you heard and saw; recall your reactions and the reactions of those around you. We call this technique triggering; that is, evoking past images and emotions of success will trigger the same type of attitude in the present. Great actors use the technique. They evoke the emotions necessary for their role by reviving similar emotions they have experienced in their own lives. Carry with you, always, your positive pictures and emotions from the past. You will need them in order to resist the negativity you are bound to encounter almost everywhere you turn in this essentially negative-thinking world.

## 7. Visualize

Most confident people have developed their confidence in a given area as a result of having worked in it over an extended period of time. It is logical that a young salesperson calling on a prospect for the first time will not have as much confidence as a seasoned salesperson. However, using the techniques of visualization and emotional memory can significantly expedite the confidence-gaining process. As we said in chapter two, your subconscious mind stores data on all your experiences. It cannot distinguish between what you clearly visualize and what you actually see. Therefore, visualizing yourself performing effectively over and over again will cause you to feel as if you've done it many times before. When you visualize a desired state, you begin to feel at home with the image of yourself achieving that desired state. It becomes old hat, and you become an instant "old pro."

159

Visualization is simply imagining events in your mind's eye. There are two basic kinds of visualization: 1) visualizing the desired end (goal visualization); and 2) visualizing the sequence of steps required to reach the end (process visualization). Goal visualization is easier than process visualization and much more exciting. Seeing your goal achieved in your mind's eye will get you excited, motivated, and hopeful.

When we decided to buy the building where we now have our law office, it took a lot of imagination to go through with the original plan to purchase. The building was over a hundred years old, termite-infested, and run-down. It would have to be demolished. We visualized a modern office building with new red bricks and fresh paint. When we invited a client to give us his opinion of the old run-down shack we were buying, he said, "I think you're paying too much money for this. You're making a terrible mistake."

We were surprised by his response. In our mind's eye, we saw a different building from the one he saw—a gorgeous brand-new one. The client, of course, must have thought we were crazy.

It was goal visualization that motivated us to buy the property. It was excitement manufactured by the pictures we painted in our mind's eye that catapulted us forward. It persuaded us to work hard so that we could pay for the purchase and the new construction. It also helped get us through the many discouraging delays, cost overruns, and numerous disappointments that go along with such a project. The decision turned out to be a wise one. Our new building, by the way, is very similar to the one we held in our mind's eye.

Goal visualization was crucial to maintaining the proper attitude required to write this book. Often we would imagine the book completely finished, with cover and all, sitting on our office desks. This kept us excited and motivated to write when we didn't feel like doing so.

As stated in our chapter on goals, it's hard to get somewhere if you don't know where you are going. You visualize your goals for the same reasons you have goals in the first place. Nothing keeps you as focused and determined as keeping your mind's eye on the goal.

In process visualization, you see in your mind's eye the series of steps necessary to achieve your goal. Athletes have used this technique very successfully. They see themselves running downfield and catching the ball or making a move toward the basket. Studies have shown that when one vividly visualizes an athletic event such as running, the muscles in the body produce many of the same electrical and chemical reactions the actual event produces.

In some instances, people in prison have learned to type at rapid speeds without having access to a typewriter. Others have practiced the piano in their minds without having access to a real piano. When released, they were able to play as well as ever.

These phenomena are possible because the subconscious mind cannot distinguish between reality and those things vividly imagined. If you can imagine yourself performing your activity *in detail* with an *enthusiastic attitude,* this will carry over into reality. When you actually perform that activity, you will act as you did in your mental rehearsal.

## 8. Use the Subconscious

Your subconscious mind makes you act in a manner consistent with the images you choose to hold in your mind. Replace negative portraits of yourself with a portrait of the person you want to be. Visualize the person you wish to become as if you are that person already. Actively work at placing images of success in your mind. The subconscious is activated by fixed, sustained, emotion-evoking pictures. Picture yourself already in possession of your goal. What are you wearing? With whom are you associating? In what restaurants are you eating dinner? What does your home look like? The more detailed the picture, the greater the generation of a positive and confident attitude. Furthermore, by seeing the future you will generate the emotions and enthusiasm necessary to persevere through any rocky times that you encounter. It will get you through when your attitude is in danger of faltering. It will give you the desire and discipline to learn what you need to learn in order to become the person you are going to be.

It is also very effective to view actual photographs of goals. For example, if your goal is to become president of the United States, acquire photographs of the president's Oval Office and place them where you will constantly view them. Bob has these photos on his desk. Check up on the results in about twenty years.

Your conscious mind has a choice; the subconscious does not. The subconscious accepts whatever thought the conscious mind accepts. Then the subconscious acts to move you toward attaining the physical equivalent of those thoughts. The subconscious acts in this manner whether your conscious mind accepts positive attitudes or negative attitudes, positive goals or negative goals. Thus the subconscious can be used for the attainment of both good and bad. It all depends upon what you choose to consciously feed into it. The subconscious mind is like fertile soil that will accommodate whatever crop you wish to grow. You have the right to choose the crop whose harvest you will reap. However, if you do not exercise this choice, then you will be

162

subject to whatever happens to grow in the neglected soil—usually weeds. Your subconscious mind operates whether or not you intentionally program it. If you don't control the input, your subconscious mind may very well accept a negative program (remember that most of your environment is negative).

You will attract to you whatever it is that you constantly, persistently, and obsessively focus your emotionalized thoughts on—thoughts that have an emotional quality to them. Your brain is magnetized by your dominant emotionalized thoughts, and it will attract whatever you plant in your mind. This, of course, is also true of the negative thoughts. That is why it is very important to discipline yourself never to visualize, verbalize, or express in any way what you fear may happen. You must think only of what you want to occur.

Mental programming has been given a bad name by the likes of Adolf Hitler, Stalin, the KGB, the Jonestown mass suicide and other cult activities. This is unfortunate, because ignoring this vital aspect of the way human beings function leaves too much to chance. The victims of those mind abusers mentioned above were mentally controlled by someone else; they lost control of their own mental processes. Tragically, many of us volunteer for similar fates because we neglect to exercise control over our own minds. Our minds are incredibly intricate computers, programmed to succeed. Come to think of it, we were winners before we were born. Out of the multitude of sperm cells swimming toward the egg, ours won the race.

## 9. Affirmations, Inward and Outward

The idea that "we become what we think about" goes back to biblical times. And it's true. Where you are right now is due to the sum total of all your thoughts.

163

We maintain that the individual chooses what his or her thoughts will be. Therefore, each of us can think success or think failure.

## Inward Affirmations

Perhaps the most effective way to influence your attitude and what you think is by self-talk. Self-talk is simply the silent but continual verbal directions and conversations that an individual has with himself. (An excellent book on self-talk is *What to Say When You Talk to Yourself* by Shad Helmstetter.)

We talk to ourselves pretty much constantly. Unfortunately, most of what we say is negative. Researchers have found that over 75 percent of what we say to ourselves is negative, no doubt because most of what we hear from others is negative.

By simply monitoring our self-talk, we can turn the percentages around. We can say positive things 75 percent of the time. It is a lot easier than you think. Stop the negative talk, refuse to acknowledge it, and then say something positive. In time, you develop the habit of always saying positive things to yourself. Your mind will believe whatever you tell it. It will begin to act on what you tell it, creating what you want. Tell it only positive things. This positive self-talk will determine your attitude, and your attitude will determine your life.

We cannot stress enough in this book that the brain operates much like a personal computer. You are the programmer. Self-talk is the operating language. If you talk in negatives, your mind will create a negative reality. However, if you talk positively, a positive reality will follow. The beauty of this self-talk technique is that it is simple and permanent. Many of us have been psyched up at a success lecture but have found the benefits to be short-lived. In order to change, we must consistently and continually feed positive messages to our minds. Self-talk is ongoing and inevitable. Change your self-talk and you end up with an unending success lecture, leaving you permanently psyched.

Programming yourself for a positive attitude can be accomplished through affirmations. Affirmation is simply another form of talking to one's self. If we can discipline ourselves to consistently repeat positive commands to our mind—commands which conjure up definite, vivid, sensory, emotion-inducing images of the person we wish to become—we will become that person. It is helpful to simply view affirmations as repeated orders to our subconscious mind. Affirmations are the only positive means of *voluntarily choosing our personal software program;* it's a way of brainwashing *yourself.* Here are some rules for constructing the affirmative messages you are to consistently feed yourself.

*1. Your affirmations must always be expressed positively.* They must be expressed in terms of what you are to move toward, not in terms of what you're to move away from. For example, if you wanted to improve upon your bad temper, it would not be effective to say, "I do not lose my temper." You should say, instead, "I treat all others with great patience and calm." As we said in chapter two, your mind will have great trouble visualizing *not* doing something. It is much easier to visualize taking positive action.

*2. Your affirmations must refer to you.* You cannot assume what others will do, and thus you cannot affirm someone else in this way. Your affirmations must refer to your special desires, not the desires of your spouse, friends, or family. The subconscious is activated by emotionalized thoughts. It is extremely difficult to become excited or enthusiastic about goals that are not your own.

*3. Your affirmations must be specific.* You can only visualize clearly if you are fed a clearly defined and detailed vision of the person you are to become.

165

*4. Your affirmations must be phrased in the present tense.* In other words, your affirmations would state, "I *am* a confident speaker" as opposed to "I *will be* a confident speaker." Speaking in the present tense will trigger an image that, as we said earlier, will make you comfortable with the future you. This image will be accepted by the subconscious as factual, and the subconscious will cause you to act in a manner consistent with the type of person referred to in your affirmation. Remember, your subconscious mind accepts whatever you consciously feed into it. Therefore, it doesn't matter whether the statement contained in your affirmation is presently true or false. *Act as if the affirmation is about you and one day all you now say will come true.*

5. *Always carry your affirmations with you and refer to them as often as possible.* Writing them down on index cards and placing them in your wallet or purse will be a convenient way for you to do this. Repeat them as often as possible. They will abort all negative emotion. Visualize the person described in the affirmation. This will generate positive emotions, which in turn will generate faith, sustenance, and perseverance. Emotion-driven faith will act as the spark which ignites the powers of your mind.

Affirmations are simply an application of the law of suggestion, which refers to the human trait of our being influenced by constantly repeated thoughts. This law, as we have already shown, can be used for good or evil. Because many modern cult and hate organizations use precisely this technique, our society has failed to use it in a positive way. In effect, we have thrown out the baby with the bathwater.

Other examples of the power of suggestion are found in people who are induced to laugh by the laughter of others without hearing the joke. The yawning of one person in a crowd can induce yawning and sleepiness in the rest of the crowd. Faith healers can cure illness, and voodoo practitioners have been known to cure or create illness through this power of suggestion.

The law of suggestion can be classified into two types, autosuggestion and heterosuggestion. Autosuggestion or self-suggestion is exemplified by affirmations or self-talk. The individual has total control over this kind of input. You can choose what you tell yourself.

On the other hand, heterosuggestion refers to the type of input you get from the outside world—from friends and strangers alike. The world's major events have all been affected by heterosuggestion. When people begin to "fear" en masse—for example, that there is going to be a recession or even a depression—voilà, we have one! The stock market goes up and down based on the way the beliefs of some affect the beliefs of everyone. Advertising companies learned long ago that constant repetition of statements will move others to believe those statements. Thus came slogans like "Ford has a better idea," "We try harder," and "When E. F. Hutton speaks, everyone listens."

Unfortunately, many of us *allow* ourselves to be influenced by the negative suggestions of others: "You can't do that," "You can't sing," "You can't play baseball," "You can't write," "You can't act." The key word with regard to the effect of heterosuggestion is *allow*. You see, although you cannot completely control what the outside world tells you, you can control what you do with what others tell you—and in some cases you probably should tell them what they can do with it.

When we started lecturing, we were effective, but only in front of the right audience. If the audience was receptive and vibrant, so were we. We drew energy from others. A problem arose when the audience was less than receptive. In those instances, we fizzled. Eventually it occurred to us that since we were the "show," we

167

could not allow the audience to drag us down. Whether or not the audience is "up," we now know that we have to be up. When we are up, we can inspire even the most lethargic group.

By maintaining an upbeat mental attitude, those around you draw from it. People will want to be around you. If you are surrounded by negative people, they will not be able to drag you down to their level. You will uplift them. Good things will begin to happen.

You can choose either to accept and integrate and internalize the input you get, or you can totally reject it. This is why some people can rise out of poverty into lives of great accomplishment while others seem chained to the present. There would have been no *I Love Lucy* if Lucille Ball had listened to the acting "experts." Frank Sinatra would never have become a star if he had listened to the music experts in a New Jersey saloon. You would not recognize the name Joan Rivers if she had listened to her parents when they threatened to cut her off unless she abandoned her dream. *You are responsible* for what you tell yourself and for what value you place on those suggestions that are communicated to you by others.

### *Outward Affirmations*

So far we have been discussing inward affirmations—the conversations that we have with ourselves, the self-talk that we all carry on almost all the time. A few of us make outward affirmations, too, in which we state our goals to the world, sometimes in the present tense. This powerful technique, however, must be used with discretion. It is not suitable for most personality types. Success motivators are sharply divided on the propriety of telling your plans to others. One school says it's all right to do so, but only if you disclose them to carefully selected friends and confidants. Another school warns against telling anyone of your aspirations. Both schools of thought have the same rationale for their warnings. By telling others, you open yourself up to criticism and the comments of the doubters. In this sea of negativism, your optimism will drown.

We will not pass judgment either way. We will just show you how outward affirmations work. Suffice it to say that Bob uses the technique with enormous success. John, on the other hand, would never even think of using it. Only you can decide if you are comfortable with this technique.

By far the best example of outward affirmation is Mohammed Ali (aka Cassius Clay). We had the opportunity to view a TV special hosted by Marv Albert on the twenty-fifth anniversary of the first Clay/Liston fight. Watching the special was a great eye-opener, for the Singing Lawyers were still in grammar school when the fight took place. Sonny Liston, a bruiser of a fighter and the undisputed heavyweight champion of the world, was a nine-to-one favorite to annihilate a young Cassius Clay (who later changed his name to Mohammed Ali). Because of the apparent mismatch (Clay was thought to be too young and too light, since he was really a light heavyweight), most people did not wager on the outcome. Everyone knew Liston would win. The only disagreement was in what round Liston would knock out the brash young upstart.

When questioned by a reporter, Clay screamed, "I can't lose! I'm the champ!" He spoke with such conviction and excitement that the audience was jolted. Most people at the time thought Clay was an obnoxious braggart. But we see now that he was a great master of the use of outward affirmation. He accomplished just what he said he would.

Ali not only stated his intentions to the world, but he used the present tense! The present tense forces the subconscious to take whatever steps are necessary to

169

bring a hope to fruition. To put a future event in the present tense is risky. Others may view you (at best) as a dreamer or (at worst) a liar.

Bob has used this technique extensively in the building of our law practice. John, on the other hand, would cringe whenever Bob used the present tense for events that had not yet occurred. However, as these events materialized, John lost his skepticism and gained faith. The following events will show how powerful this simple (if eccentric) technique can work to produce the results that you want.

When the Singing Lawyers met at Fordham Law School in 1976, John thought Bob was a little strange. You see, whenever we went to events where people did not know us, Bob would introduce us as partners in our own law firm. This was, to say the least, a lofty claim for two freshman law students. Not only were we not lawyers, but to think that we could actually start our own practice was absurd. Classmates of ours were clamoring for high-paying positions in the elite New York City corporate law firms. The economic conditions of the time and the trend in law toward specialization did not bode well for two inexperienced general practice lawyers. John never really thought that such a partnership was possible.

When Bob made this bold assertion, people would invariably turn to John and ask, "Really, where's your office located?" John would do his best to evade the question and quickly change the subject. Later he would grab Bob by the arm and say, "How could you concoct such a story? Are you crazy?" Crazy or not, just three years from graduation, we did in fact start our own law firm. The seed that had been planted in law school had germinated.

Some time after we had started our own practice, John's father joined the firm, bringing added experience, expertise, and stability. Since we were growing, we decided it would be advantageous to try to buy a building. This was a theory that John's father held for many years. He often counseled his clients to buy the building their business was housed in. Too many good businesses are forced out because of unpredictable landlords and escalating rent. Many of John's father's clients are wealthy today not because of their business but because, on his advice, they are owners of real estate that has appreciated in value.

For us, the idea had some major opportunities—that is, problems. First, there were no buildings for sale in Great Neck—at least none that we could afford. After months of looking, we were about to give up. Then one day a client approached John, congratulating him on purchasing a building. "When are you going to move into your new building?" New building? We weren't even close to finding one to negotiate on. John smiled politely and excused himself. Embarrassed, he found Bob and said, "Are you crazy?" Exactly one month later, we signed a contract to purchase perhaps the only building in Great Neck that was for sale in our price range. It was a great opportunity that just came out of the blue. It has helped us enormously in the development of our practice.

A few years later, Bob came up with the idea of the Singing Lawyers. What made him even more of a nut was that he would often tell people that we were going to appear on Channel 7 ABC TV. People would call John and ask him when the story was going to be aired. After adroitly sidestepping the question, John would confront Bob with "Are you crazy?" A short time later, CNN did a story on the Singing Lawyers at the Nassau County Supreme Court. While the filming was going on, a Channel 7 ABC reporter approached us for their own story. We appeared on ABC (as well as on many other stations thereafter).

Bob is still at it. When the Singing Lawyers appeared on the Wil Shriner Show on NBC TV in 1988, Mr. Shriner asked Bob his ultimate goal. Bob said, "I want to be the first Jewish president of the United States." Saying this in ordinary company is brazen enough— but on national television? Now that's chutzpa! After the show, John grabbed Bob by the arm and said, "Are you . . . looking for a running mate?"

As we have said, this technique is not for everyone. You must be willing to overcome the ridicule of others. Many people will think that you are conceited, deluded, not to be trusted. You must be able to make your affirmations with total self-confidence. If you do, then no matter what other things people may think about you, they will look upon you with a degree of respect and admiration. And they will be astonished as the things you predict come to pass.

Going public with your intentions puts pressure on you to achieve them. You don't want to appear foolish or give others the satisfaction of seeing you fail. As you know from previous chapters, merely writing down a goal privately shows a great commitment, and your mind will create the reality necessary to achieve that goal. How much more of a commitment is required to tell the whole world!

## 10. Mental Music—Song of Success

Self-talk is an extremely powerful programming technique. Self-song, or mental music, is even more effective. What is self-song? It occurs any time you sing or hum, or merely hear a tune in your head. Self-song can be one of two types: music heard—that is, music that you sing or hum; or silent music—that is, music that is played silently in your mind's ear.

Self-song works for the same reasons that self-talk works. However, music gives an added dimension. Re-

172

searchers have found that certain kinds of music aid in learning. Many professional athletes use music to psych themselves up into higher levels of performance. Walter Payton, the former Chicago Bears football star who ran for more yards than anyone in National Football League history, used music before a game to help produce the attitude needed to play professional football.

Music can help trigger the mental state you desire. If you want to get motivated to exercise, you might play the theme from *Rocky*. If you don't have access to a tape recorder, you could play the melody in your head. If you are fearful in certain situations, you might whistle a happy tune, as Anna did in *The King and I.*

Again, *you* control the record player. If you play the blues in your mind, you'll feel unhappy. If you play an upbeat melody, you'll be optimistic. Making mental music helps make your attitude as well. It is helpful to start the day with an upbeat song. It can set the tone for the entire day. You'll be surprised how this actually helps you to be happy. Each song done by the Singing Lawyers is associated with a particular success concept contained in this book.

Unfortunately, many people are very hard on themselves when it comes to their own singing. They will seldom sing within earshot of others. That's why silent singing is important. You can sing in your mind's ear, and no one can criticize you. To be honest, though, once you sing silently, you will have to be on guard. Sometimes without warning, your silent singing can turn into real crooning. In that case, try to stay on key!

## 11. Constructive Reading

Unfortunately, most people stop reading when they graduate from school. Oh, they'll read an occasional newspaper or magazine, but few will read a book from cover to cover. It's a shame, because reading is to your mind what exercise is to your body. Reading just one serious book each month will give you a great deal of knowledge and even elevate you to the upper echelons of educated society. Of course, what you read is just as important as what self-talk you use or whom you associate with. Reading cheap fiction or pornography is not likely to develop your mind. More likely it will hurt you.

Other than books in those fields that interest you, we recommend two kinds of reading for success: 1) biographies and autobiographies of great people; and 2) self-help success books. It's obvious why you should read self-help success books. They will give you the techniques needed to succeed. They are written by positive, upbeat people. As you read, the enthusiasm will be contagious. You will inculcate positive thoughts. Unfortunately, this great idea of success literature is never mentioned during formal education. We have each had about twenty years of formal education. Not once was any success writer alluded to in any class. What a tragedy.

Just as important is the reading of biographies and autobiographies of great people. Benjamin Franklin once said that the next best thing to experience is reading about another's experience. If you want to be successful in a particular field, find out those who have been successful in those fields and read their stories. You can learn from their mistakes and be inspired by their triumphs. Most great people have faced great adversity. Their stories will show how small your obstacles are by comparison. Learn from them and do what they did.

Set aside a certain number of hours a week for reading. Make a list of books in these categories that you think will be helpful and start reading.

## 12. Positive Quotations List

Self-talk is a very effective tool. However, sometimes we respond better to what others say. Perhaps the power of suggestion from others is so effective because we have been brought up to respect figures of authority. If you tell yourself that you have unlimited potential, that is effective. To hear it from a great historical figure makes it even more convincing.

That is why you should keep a journal of positive quotations. Add to this list at your leisure. Review it often. Commit the quotations to memory. Say them throughout the day. You'll experience an enormous change of attitude. These powerful words will become part of you. You will consciously and subconsciously draw upon this deep well of positive thoughts whenever you need to.

When you feel like quitting a project, recall the words of Winston Churchill, "Never give up. Never, never give up." When you feel tired and lacking in energy, recite "But they that wait upon the Lord shall renew their strength; they shall mount up with wings as eagles; they shall run, and not be weary; and they shall walk, and not faint" (Isaiah 40:31).

The sources for this positive thought list should be those which are most important to you. The Bible is the best source of positive practical advice. It is God's operator's manual for life.

By selecting quotations you can relate to, you will slowly develop your personal arsenal. Your own philosophy of life will emerge. In time, you can begin writing your own quotations, building a crescendo of positive thought energy that will keep propelling you into positive action.

## 13. Personal Positive Memory Bank

Perhaps even more powerful than a positive quotations list is your own positive recall list, a list made up of those select positive statements others have made about you. Nothing makes you feel better or gives you more exhilaration than a sincere compliment from another. It's one thing to tell yourself that you're fantastic or to read a quotation from a prominent person. It's quite another thing to have someone else, whether a stranger or a friend, tell you that you are terrific. There is something in all of us that screams out "I am special." When another person acknowledges this, the floodgates open and a river of exultant emotion pours out. Nothing is more powerful in changing your state of mind than an unsolicited compliment from another person.

Unfortunately, after receiving such compliments, we often dismiss them and fail to dwell on them. A bit embarrassed by another person's ability to evoke such powerful feelings in us, we quickly change the subject. It is truly amazing how people tend to focus on negative things that are said about them. Not wanting to be conceited, they dwell on the negative, not the positive.

All of us can recall times in our life when someone said something extremely flattering. It might have been when a teacher read your composition as the best in the class. Or when a baseball coach said you had the best attitude on the team. Parents might have told you how proud of you they were. A date may have remarked how attractive you looked. Recall how good you felt after hearing these words. Unfortunately, we tend to forget such moments. Just as we told you earlier to re-live successful experiences, so you should re-experience the positive words.

Make a list of such compliments. Add to the list. Put the words in quotation marks with the name and position of the person who said them. Seeing the words on paper will not only help remind you; it will also add tremendous legitimacy to the words. By reading and rereading this list, you will saturate your mind with healthy doses of positive self-imagery. Since we become what we think about, our self-image will reflect the tone of these positive statements.

Keep the list handy. If you read it before bedtime, your mind will dwell on the positive. Reading the list in the morning can set a positive tone for the rest of the day. Referring to the list through the day can help fend off down times and help you maintain a healthy perspective.

## 14. Positive Physiology

We must not forget how vital our physical bodies are in determining and controlling our attitudes. The relatively new theory of Neuro-Linguistic Programming (NLP) has brought this back to our attention. Part of NLP is monitoring your physiology to produce the desired emotional state. Actually, there is nothing really new about it. The principles of controlling your physiology to produce positive emotions is as old as mankind.

There is a reason why West Point Cadets are drilled in proper posture. In wartime, chiefs and generals always carried themselves erect with heads held high. The military uniform itself plays a role in engendering the fighting spirit.

Teachers in elementary school have their pupils stand and stretch during the day in order to improve circulation and attitude. A baseball player is told to keep his chin up after a strikeout so as not to yield to the onset of negative emotions. Very few heads of state are "slouchers." Generally, regardless of their height or build, they stand with their shoulders square and their heads up. If you are a leader, you must act the part.

Recently a client who had been injured in an auto accident came to us. The accident had triggered a severe depression in her. It turned out that she actually had been chronically depressed most of her life. Years of psychotherapy had produced questionable results. We noted her slouched position and her frequent sighing. We asked her how she would stand and breathe if she were happy. Then we asked her to physically demonstrate her "happy" posture. Once she had established she could do this, we asked her to try moving and breathing this way for an entire day. At present, she reports feeling improved. Did positive physiology solve all her underlying problems? Of course not, but it is obviously preferable to negative physiology.

Every day when you wake up, stand and stretch. Look in the mirror, stand straight, and keep your head up. You can then meet the day with self-confidence.

In addition, stay in physical shape. Regular aerobic exercise makes you look and feel better. We both have regular exercise schedules. We find ourselves irritable and out of sync if we do not exercise regularly. Dr. Kenneth Cooper believes that many of our social ills—depression, lack of self-esteem, drugs, and so on—could be avoided if we all followed a regular program of aerobic exercise. He may be right.

## 15. Nutrition for a Positive Mental Attitude

No discussion about attitude and mental state would be complete without acknowledging the importance of nutrition. The problem is that the field of nutrition has always been and continues to be contradictory. So-called experts disagree on even the most basic points.

In addition, nutritional therapy has often been tied to weight loss. Therefore, many questionable methods are espoused to achieve the goal of losing weight while ignoring the more important goal of eating for health and well-being.

The term *diet* itself has been misused. Instead of describing the permanent mode of eating, it has come to mean a temporary quick-fix method of losing a few pounds.

You may be wondering what the Singing Lawyers know about nutrition. Well, nutrition has been a lifelong study for John, who was a lecturer for the Pritikin Better Health Program in Great Neck, New York. But this is not a nutrition book, so we will just give you some basics that will help you maintain the good health necessary for a good attitude.

The body's basic nutrient is oxygen. Therefore, anything that increases the supply of oxygen to your tissues will help your body work at its maximum potential. Not surprisingly, proper breathing is essential. Proper breathing is deep breathing from the diaphragm. Diaphragmatic breathing serves two functions: 1) it infuses oxygen into the bloodstream; and 2) it aids the body's immune system by stimulating the cleaning of toxins from your body.

This dual function, nourishing and cleansing, keeps the cells in peak operating condition. Practice deep breathing several times throughout the day. Of course, engaging in aerobic exercise also helps nourish and cleanse the cells. Breathing is so crucial to bodily health and mental state that it is the basic foundation of yoga.

We do not want to impede the flow of oxygen to the cells. Therefore, we must eat foods that do not disrupt our circulatory system. Generally speaking, our diets should be high in complex carbohydrates (grains and vegetables) and low in foods containing high levels of protein, fat, cholesterol, and sugar. When complex carbohydrates metabolize, the by-products are carbon dioxide and water, which are both easily eliminated. The by-products of protein metabolism are urea, nitrogen, and nitric acid, which are poisons. This is why you are required to drink a lot of

179

water while on a high protein diet. The water helps neutralize and eliminate these toxins.

Another advantage to eating complex carbohydrates is that they are naturally high in fiber. This aids elimination and prevents the buildup of toxins in the body. They also tend to be water-rich foods that aid the circulatory system.

When you eat foods high in fat, the fat enters the bloodstream and coats the oxygen-carrying red blood cells, thus hindering their effectiveness. It's difficult for the oxygen to get to the cells. That is why you feel so sluggish after consuming a large meal high in fats.

Eating foods rich in sugar is also unwise. Since simple sugars require practically no digestion, the body acts fast to convert this sudden rush of energy into storage. The storage is fat. Levels of triglyceride (fat in the blood) are raised, causing problems in your system. In addition, you experience a high from this sudden surge of energy and a real low soon thereafter.

When you eat foods high in cholesterol, your serum cholesterol levels rise, and the excess cholesterol is deposited in your arteries. This leads to all sorts of diseases of the cardiovascular system (the number one cause of death in this country). Cholesterol and fat have become a modern American plague. Acting together, they cause more deaths than all other causes combined.

What foods contain fat and cholesterol? Any foods that come from animal sources—all meat, eggs, cheeses, and other dairy products. The foods that are high in cholesterol are also high in fat content. You can enjoy these foods if the fat content is lowered. Thus, low-fat dairy products and lean meats are acceptable, if not eaten in excess. No foods which are derived from plants contain any cholesterol, and the vast majority are very low in fat.

There is no better way to keep a clear head than by eating a diet of complex carbohydrates. Eating complex car-

180

bohydrates such as breads, cereals, rice, and pasta insures a steady stream of glucose and oxygen to the brain. You will be keeping mind-slowing poisons out of your body, and you will be supplying it with high energy. Studies of those populations that enjoy the longest life spans show that they eat this way as well as engage in regular exercise.

Generally, once a food has been processed, its very nature has been changed, and the delicate ratio of carbohydrates, fat, and protein is altered. Corn in its natural state is a complex carbohydrate and an excellent food. However, processing it into corn oil changes things. Now it is no longer a balanced food, because corn oil is almost pure fat. It takes many ears of corn to make a tablespoon of corn oil. Oils and oil products, which are fats, should be used sparingly. They tend to be high in polyunsaturated fats which, when oxidized, produce harmful substances. Certain degenerative diseases, as well as premature aging, can result.

Our bodies were made to digest complex carbohydrates. However, when these whole foods are processed, many of the vitamins, minerals, and fiber are destroyed or removed in the process. They are turned into artificial foods, that is, sugar, fats, and oils. Our bodies are unable to assimilate these concentrated forms, and problems develop.

It is difficult to maintain a positive mental attitude if you are not healthy. Good health, in most cases, results from lifestyle choices that you make. If you take care of your body by eating the right foods and by proper regular exercise, your body will take care of you.

## 16. Use Image Restructuring

A very effective way to combat any negative situation is to restructure what you see. Of course, the actual picture remains the same; only your perception of it

181

changes. As we've said, your mental state is determined not so much by what is happening around you as by your reaction to what is happening. Image restructuring is powerful. It can turn very upsetting circumstances into relatively easy ones.

For example, John was representing a buyer at a very tense real estate closing. Closings generally are rather calm and uneventful. However, in this case there was a serious disagreement between the buyer and the seller. While they argued and negotiated, the seller's attorney was putting on a show, ranting and raving and casting menacing glances toward John's side of the table. Even when the parties had reached a compromise, the seller's attorney continued to scream and threaten.

In order to keep his cool and save the deal, John did some image restructuring. He pictured the seller's lawyer in a clown costume licking a big lollipop. The situation didn't change, but the way in which John represented the situation to himself *did* change. The seller's attorney couldn't make a dent in John's calm demeanor, and the parties came to an agreement.

The next time someone is screaming at you, whether an irate driver or spouse or customer, try this restructuring. Imagine that there is another person standing next to you. Pretend the antagonist is doing the yelling at this imaginary friend. Sympathize with this friend and feel bad for the ill treatment he or she is receiving. You'll find it impossible to get upset with the screamer. Since you are not reacting to the yelling, the yelling will cease.

It's a foolproof way of defusing a high-pitched argument. You can then rationally discuss the problem.

Just how you restructure the input is up to you. You may envision the offending person as standing only a few inches tall or speaking in a sped-up voice—like a chipmunk. You may picture him as standing two blocks away, or you can see him as an infant holding a rattle.

182

By remaining in control, you will have a calming effect on the person or persons doing the screaming. You will not only control your own attitude but will change his mental state as well.

Image restructuring is crucial in some businesses. The cardinal rule of any retail or service business is "The customer is always right." Never get upset with customers or clients. Listen to them, stay calm, and eventually they will change their demeanor. In fact, they will often feel a bit embarrassed by their behavior and will end up apologizing. You'll defuse a difficult situation and keep the customer as well.

### 17. Make It a Habit

We are creatures of habit. Therefore, once something becomes a habit, it becomes easy. Like all attitudes, positive mental attitude is learned. It must go through four stages of learning:

1. Unconscious Incompetence ( you don't know that you don't know)
2. Conscious Incompetence (you know you don't know so you consciously attempt to learn, but you are not very good at it)
3. Conscious Competence (you make an effort to perform the task and succeed, but it takes conscious effort)
4. Unconscious Competence (you can perform the task well without even thinking about it; very little effort is required)

Learning to ride a bicycle is a good example. Until you try it, you don't realize that you can't do it (unconscious incompetence). When you first attempt it, you can't do it (conscious incompetence). Eventually,

America Doesn't Owe You a Living

with great effort, you can do it (conscious competence). Finally, you are able to hop on the bicycle and ride well without giving it a second thought (unconscious competence).

The same steps apply to the development of attitude. First, you must realize that your attitude needs improvement. Then you must work at it until you are positive by habit, until by nature your attitude is always up. Train yourself to generate excitement and positiveness until others start reacting to you, instead of you to them.

184

# 6

# CHANNELING SEXUAL ENERGY

What you think about constantly will be what drives you. If you constantly think about the pursuit of the opposite sex, that is exactly what will dominate your life. This may be why young people who have a stable married and family life usually move onto the fast track of their careers earlier than some single people, who more often spend their evenings on the fast track of singles bars and clubs. Successful people have managed to transfer or *channel* their sexual nature into their drive to obtain their career goals. Having a highly sexual nature, in itself, is neither good nor bad. However, the way in which it is expressed can be potentially good or bad. When drawn upon in such a way as to debilitate one's energy in essential areas, it is bad. Not only does it dissipate your energy, but in dominating your thoughts it dominates your life. We know that we usually get what we constantly think about. Therefore, constant dwelling on sex may produce heightened sexual activity. But be forewarned. Sexual promiscuity is no longer simply immoral; it can be deadly. Consequently, sexual channeling is now much more than a means to success; it's also a matter of self-defense against deadly disease.

A more fulfilling life as a human being, and not just a sexual being, can be achieved if one uses the tremendous storehouse of energy contained in one's natural sex drive. Channeling this drive can ignite your creative flames. Channeling your sex drive is certainly easier said than done, but if you can apply to your career goals the same passion and urgency evoked in the pursuit of the opposite sex, you can set the world on fire.

## The Fiction of Sexual Addiction

Your sexual drive is within your complete control. Once again, it's a matter of choice. As we stated in chapter one, only you are responsible for making that choice.

We are now living in an era in which every perverse form of behavior is excused under the rubric of addiction. Just as those who choose to take drugs, betray their families, or even commit crimes, have been assigned "victim" status, the sexually irresponsible are being labeled "sex addicts" by some psychologists. As reported in *Time* magazine (June 4, 1990), these psychologists say that chemical imbalances and other factors control the addict's behavior. It is a short leap from this to argue that sex addicts should never be blamed for their behavior, no matter who is hurt by it.

We even have Sexaholics Anonymous groups springing up like weeds. You don't have to look too far to see the dangers inherent in this philosophy. Next, we can expect rapists and child abusers using this defense in court, spawning a new legal specialty. After all, how can we punish someone for biological predetermination?

This entire movement is a fraud. Sexual promiscuity is easy to figure out. It feels good, so despite physical and emotional risks people engage in it.

Sex feels good because that is how the Creator intended it. Men and women were to be fruitful and multiply. They were not, however, given a license to act without regard to responsibility, obligation, and God-centered morality.

The so-called sexual revolution has left countless numbers of women and children in poverty. It has now become a sign of status for older, wealthy male executives to trade their wives in for a new model as they would a car; this trend was even featured as the cover story of *Fortune* magazine. Although it is certainly the case that wealthy men can afford to support their ex-wives and children, it is equally true that many others cannot do so. When we glamorize this type of behavior, we encourage people of all economic groups to emulate it. As a result, innocent children and their mothers are left out in the cold financially and, more importantly, emotionally.

We must stop providing excuses and alibis in the form of genes, environment, or addiction. To provide this easy way out is to perpetuate the behavior. Even in these permissive times, deep down, people know that this behavior is wrong. They have not completely forgotten the Ten Commandments. Therefore, they look for any rationale to assuage their guilt. The pop psychologists and their addiction theories are just the excuse the deviants need. Men and women of common sense should give these pop psychologists a one-way ticket back to Psychology 101.

## Passion Ignites Charisma

It has been our experience that most successful people are very highly sexed. These people, particularly those in the sales-oriented business, have what is commonly known as charisma. Charisma is a polite

187

way of referring to what is really sexual energy. When you're at a cocktail party, in school, on the job, at a meeting, at a wedding, at a convention, any type of function where there are many people present, look around you. Among all of the ordinary flock, you may see a few people who glow with charisma. Objective observation reveals that they do not necessarily have superior physiques, figures, or facial features, but somehow an aura emanates from them.

One often hears news commentators and other people in the media speak of certain public figures having charisma. From them, one may be given the impression that charisma is something these public figures were just born with. This is wrong. Everyone has charisma; it exists within each person. Each person is a sexual being, and a sex drive is just another one of the powerful energies that make up a human being. Charismatic people are people who are in touch with the charisma within them.

How an individual perceives himself is known as his self-image. The reasons we view ourselves as we do may be buried in early childhood. Psychiatrists and psychologists can possibly help us recall them. However, that is not the function of this book. Our purpose is to motivate you to make your life what you want it to be. Forget Freud and your mother. It is still possible to turn your life around by giving attention to your future, even if you don't plumb all the secrets of your past. Once you do that, you will view yourself in a better light, and the way in which you view yourself is the way in which others will view you.

Observe successful people, and you will see that this is true. Watch the way they carry themselves; observe their mannerisms, listen to their voices. As you watch other people, you will become increasingly proficient at analyzing them. Eventually this ability to analyze others will enable you to use them as a barometer to measure your progress. This does not mean that you measure your success by that of others. Success is a highly personal concept that entails your becoming the best that *you* can possibly be. Nevertheless, there is much to be gained from the careful observation of human behavior.

## Sex As a Motivator

Let's begin by observing that sex plays a large part in the lives of most people. Man, in his basic nature, has not changed much from the Garden of Eden. Just as early man hunted and used his hunting prowess to impress the opposite sex, people today (though not hunting for food), often initially seek success in order to impress members of the opposite sex. Jewelry, fancy clothes, and expensive cars are all means of demonstrating to the opposite sex one's prowess in the "civilized jungle."

We have spoken with many entertainers and other public figures who entered their high-profile careers as a means of attracting members of the opposite sex. A good friend of ours, as a teenager, was not as popular with the opposite sex as he would have liked. For some reason, which only his psychoanalyst knows (but won't tell him), our friend was very shy when it came to approaching women. His shyness and lack of self-confidence were indicative of the way he felt about himself and affected the way women viewed him.

One day at a school dance he made an important discovery. He noted that members of the disco band were surrounded by beautiful women despite the fact that the band members were Quasimodo look-alikes. The women listened in ecstasy as the band played. Our friend finally realized what it was about these guys that

189

drove these women into a frenzy: they were musicians. In this high-profile arena, they were doing something well, something that made them stand out. Though at first glance they were homely, the young men had appeal because they excelled at something—making music. Women who were attracted to the music were consequently attracted to them.

Today, after years of singing lessons, our friend works as a professional singer. There is no guarantee that he will ever become a star; however, he does something very well—something that makes him stand out among most other people. He now attracts to himself more than his share of the people he desires.

The point is not that one has to become a singer to be attractive. The point is that, with all your diversified talents, you can become exceptional at something—tennis, golf, music, writing, public speaking, bodybuilding, your business. When you develop your talent fully, people will notice you.

You do not have to have good looks to be successful with the opposite sex. Woody Allen attracts as many women as Robert Redford. Mickey Rooney certainly had no more problem than Tom Selleck in finding attractive and appealing mates. The reason that Woody Allen and Mickey Rooney are attractive to women is that they are extremely talented and witty. Barbra Streisand certainly lacks classic good looks and yet, due largely to her immense talent, she is considered extremely sensual and charismatic.

## Shift the Focus

We have observed that accomplished people rarely achieve great success until they are in their fifties. One apparent reason for this is the preoccupation of young people with the pursuit of the opposite sex. It is not easy to arise at 6 A.M. to meet the challenges of a budding career when one has gone to bed at 5 A.M. However, this preoccupation of young people is not a complete waste. They learn much about themselves and others during the course of the chase.

It has been said that selling in the business world is really just a different form of seduction. The same techniques that succeed with members of the opposite sex are identical to those required to succeed in any other area. Self-examination, self-development, observation, persistence, planning, visualization, and imagination all play a strong role in the pursuit of the opposite sex. They are also essential for success in any endeavor.

If we take a brief look at an exercise of these principles, the analogy is readily apparent. An individual tends to be very self-critical when viewing himself in terms of how he shapes up in the dating game. One worries if he weighs too much or has other negative physical characteristics. People spend extraordinary amounts of time and money deciding how they should look and then taking the steps necessary to improve their appearance.

Most of us recall the Charles Atlas cartoon advertisement. A young skinny runt is on the beach with his girlfriend when a muscular bully comes over and kicks sand in his face. The slightly built man dares not stand up to his muscle-bound adversary. The moral of the story is exhibited when his girl leaves in search of a "real man." Later on, after developing his body, the young man overpowers the bully and wins back his maiden. Believe it or not, this advertisement propelled many a "skinny runt" onto the road to fitness and bodybuilding.

Carrying this concept a step further, we observe that people spend billions of dollars each year on consumer goods aimed at improving their appearance—cosmet-

191

ics, contact lenses, shampoos, designer eyeglasses, hair-pieces, hair transplants—and a fortune in medical costs for plastic surgery. These are all outgrowths of this tremendous *drive* to be perceived as attractive.

If one would only channel into career goals a frac-tion of the time and effort expended in undergoing the self-examination and self-improvement of one's looks, succeeding would be a lead-pipe cinch. Fortunately, at-tracting members of the opposite sex and attracting success are achieved by a similar process.

This truth is clearly illustrated in the area of physi-ology. How does one carry himself when he wishes to impress members of the opposite sex? Is he slouched, stooped, or slumped? Are his eyes glued to the floor? Certainly not, not if he wishes to impress a woman. And not if he wishes to close his sale. Instead, he walks with his head erect, his shoulders squared; he moves with an air of confidence and grace reminiscent of Fred Astaire or Ginger Rogers. It really doesn't matter whether the field of play has changed from the bed-room to the boardroom. The same presence is required.

How one carries himself will dictate how he will carry off his aims vis-à-vis the people he deals with. Studies have shown that most communication is non-verbal. It is not what you say but how you say it (and the posture you are in when you say it). Furthermore, your physiology will strongly influence what you think and feel about yourself. Other people will mirror those feelings. Jut as confidence is contagious, so is its lack. If you are slouched over with your head down, you will feel insecure, and others will feel insecure about you. Consider some successful past and present political fig-ures—Ronald Reagan, John F. Kennedy, Margaret Thatcher, Elizabeth Dole, and Martin Luther King Jr. Are they—were they—slouches? No way! You cannot be an effective leader and communicator without mastering your posture and body language. Such mastery is part and parcel of acting and looking like the person you desire to be.

The pursuit of the opposite sex and the pursuit of success also have much in common when it comes to communication and verbal skills. In order to succeed in the dating game or in business, you must develop a sales pitch. The same key elements apply. You must exhibit interest in the other person and generate excitement and enthusiasm. You must show concern for the needs of the prospective client and demonstrate why your product is the obvious solution. If you can do this, you can sell yourself—or anything else.

In order to attract members of the opposite sex, you need to develop a keen sense of observation. The same is necessary to attract success. You will have to be able to pick out those people who show an interest in what you have to offer. You will tend to gravitate towards those places and people where the odds are best for meeting potential customers. As a result of sexual channeling, you'll spend time with people who can make a difference in your career just as you would go to a coed health club to meet members of the opposite sex. Regardless of the field of play, you'll focus in on your prospects.

Just as one plans events during courtship, you will plan strategy when courting a potential customer. In the same manner that you visualize conversations with the object of your affection, you will visualize conversations with your potential customers. (Of course, the contents of the conversation might differ a bit.)

Visualization plays a major role in our relations with the opposite sex and also in our career goals. Again, the contents of your career visualization might differ a bit from your sexual visualization. However, the effect will be the same. Visualization will help you attain your desired end.

193

In short, people succeed in their relations with the opposite sex, just as they succeed in their careers, when they utilize the success techniques of self-evaluation, self-mastery, and visualization. They are able to obtain mastery in an area of life in which they have a naturally strong desire or drive to achieve a result—in the one case, mating. Their intense desire drives them to *think* constantly and consistently about obtaining the fruits or results of that desire. As a consequence, the object of their thoughts is obtained.

Shift your focus from sex to success and you will call upon the very same mechanisms to aid you in the achievement of an equally satisfying, though different, result.

## Sex As High-Octane Fuel

Sexual desire is one of the strongest drives we find in the human species. People have been moved to great feats of bravery or cunning, honesty or deceit, and good or evil in the pursuit of the objects of their desire. Since desire is the power plant that fuels our quest for success, the powerful sex desire is virtually unstoppable. Sexual desire is a fact of nature that cannot be erased.

Prizefighters have sometimes been told to refrain from sex prior to a big fight in order to channel their energy into winning the match. Constructive sexual channeling has led to inspirational leadership and accomplishment of great men and women throughout our history. Unchanneled sexual desire led to the downfall of such notables as Gary Hart, Jimmy Swaggert, and Jim and Tammy Bakker.

A goal can move one in the direction of its attainment only if the goal is emotionalized. The emotions of sex and love are highly powerful stimulants that will breathe life into your goals and make them reality. Sexual energy will inspire the faculties of the creative imagina-

194

tion. Learn to control your drives and draw upon your urges for strength and energy in the pursuit of longer-lasting goals, and you will indeed be a force to be reckoned with. The sex urge is a far more effective stimulant of creative energy than drugs or alcohol. Although some of our most creative writers, composers, and authors were alcoholics or drug addicts, these artificial stimulants often led to their demise and may even have stunted their genius. Nature's inventions are always superior to the artificial concoctions of man. Use of alcohol or drugs may temporarily stimulate one's creative abilities, relieve tensions, and break down inhibitions; but the positive effects are short-lived and the negative effects permanent. We have ourselves had the experience of singing after taking a drink and feeling, while we were performing, that our performances were superior. A subsequent tape playback revealed slightly off-key notes and slurred phrasing.

## Enthusiasm Is Contagious

Top salespeople effectively channel sexual energy into their greatest asset: enthusiasm. Enthusiasm is highly contagious and can be used for good or evil. Leaders in all walks of life use enthusiasm to inspire their followers to pursue worthy objectives. On the other hand, many dictators have used it to inspire their people to evil ends; Adolf Hitler was an extremely enthusiastic salesman.

Salespeople who are enthusiastic about their product are more likely to produce enthusiasm in their prospective customers. Observe any sales presentation, whether it be the sale of a product, the sale of a political candidate, or the sale of an idea. The best-informed speaker will quickly put an audience to sleep if he fails to exude great enthusiasm for his subject. On the other hand, a speaker totally devoid of substance can ignite flames in his audience by virtue of his enthusiastic delivery. We see this demonstrated every day in both private and public sectors.

Any real estate salesperson will tell you that a prospective home buyer makes his decision on the basis of emotion and enthusiasm. Ted Metalios, owner/broker of Century 21 Metalios in Jackson Heights, New York (the most successful franchise in the Century 21 system), says, "Buyers always buy on the basis of emotion, whereas sellers sell on the basis of logic [$$$$]." Political pollsters and analysts have concluded that, to a large measure, the electorate votes according to its *feelings* about a candidate. This is known as the so-called "likability factor." Ronald Reagan was an extremely likable candidate. He had emotion, sincerity, and humility, and used self-deprecatory humor about his age to tremendous advantage.

Many pundits believe that the loser in the 1988 election destroyed any chance he had when he delivered an emotionless response to a debate question referring to whether the death penalty should be used on the hypothetical murderer of his own wife. The loser was seen as a computer-like technocrat without passion or purpose. In fact, he himself stated that the presidential campaign was not about ideas and values, but about some sort of robotic competence. His lack of emotion was perceived as a lack of strong values and principles. After all, why would someone buy from (or vote for) someone who doesn't enthusiastically believe in what he is selling?

## Sex Is Here to Stay

The sex drive is not exclusively either good or bad. Humans are not only sexual beings; they are also naturally selfish creatures. In other words, humans act out of their own self-interest. This is also neither good nor bad; it is just a fact. This trait of selfishness is good when, through the American system of capitalism, we are driven to produce things that ultimately benefit all of humanity. It is good when, out of a feeling of *personal* satisfaction, we help others less fortunate than ourselves. However, make no mistake, charity is still a selfish act, because the giver receives the personal benefit of self-satisfaction and moral well-being.

This trait of selfishness becomes evil only when a person helps himself at the expense of, or to the detriment of, his family, company, team, or society.

Likewise, when sexual energy is channeled into creating new ideas and products that benefit humanity, the sex drive is certainly a good trait. It is only when it is used to spread disease or debilitate the individual or family morally or physically that it becomes evil. As is true of all human traits, the sex drive can push one to great accomplishment if it is harnessed in the way a dam harnesses the energy of powerful flowing rivers. However, if the dam breaks and sex energy runs wild, it can be a most destructive force.

## Finding the Right Mate

The destructive potential of human sexuality can be eliminated when you find a mate who will inspire you emotionally and physically, one who will complement your values and goals. It is not important that you and your mate be alike in temperament. As a matter of fact, the most opposite of temperaments form the most effective teams. As the saying goes, "Opposites attract." It is essential, though, that the values you and your mate hold be completely in harmony. You must have the same sense of what is right and wrong. This is where

197

honest evaluation, as opposed to wishful thinking about yourself and your prospective mate, is essential.

Anyone who enters a relationship expecting the other person to change his or her ingrained ideas, attitudes, and lifestyle is in for a rude awakening. Such people inevitably wind up in a divorce, leaving only the lawyers living happily ever after. Consider how difficult it is to change yourself. If it takes so much for you to change yourself, how in the world can you ever stake your life on changing someone else? Only those who know themselves will be able to choose life partners who will work together with them to build a fulfilling life.

Many people fall in love because they want to be "in love." They think that someone else is going to be responsible for rescuing them from a life devoid of direction and definite purpose. They think that all will be right with the world if they can somehow meet Mr. or Ms. Right. The fact is that Mr. or Ms. Right is you. What you think and feel about yourself will cause either Mr. Wrong or Mr. Right to come into your life. If you can't make yourself happy, don't expect anyone else to do it for you; and don't expect to do it for anyone else.

## Avoiding Sexual Detours

Sexual channeling is not easy to accomplish. As in any other area where the rewards are great, sexual channeling requires discipline and the ability to forgo immediate gratification.

As people become more successful, their sexual charisma increases; therefore, the opposite sex is more attracted to them. It is at this point, when one's career is on the rise, that failure to exercise self-discipline and proper channeling of sex energy can trip one up on the way to the top. One-time presidential front-runner Senator Gary Hart provided an excellent demonstra-

198

tion of this truth. His presidential aspirations were dashed on the rocks by his inability to channel his sexual energies into his political career. There is no need to look further than Chappaquiddick to see that even the most rich and powerful are vulnerable to the consequences of their weaknesses.

Many a promising career has been knocked off course by indiscreet office relationships, romances with clients, and liaisons that compromise family life and business life. On the other hand, many a career has been enhanced by a stable and strong loving relationship.

Despite its difficulties, sexual channeling must be mastered. One practical means of doing this is found in the chapter on goals. Whenever a potentially destructive inclination arises, it is extremely effective to focus on your ultimate long-term goals. This will serve to remind you that the short-term gain is not worth the long-term pain.

By the way, do not make the mistake of thinking that the authors recommend *total* sexual channeling; between us, we have helped bring six beautiful children into this world. By channeling our sexual energy, however, we have managed to make all the fruits of our sexuality unqualifiably positive and beautiful.

# 7

# DETERMINATION AND PERSISTENCE

Determination and persistence are the sine qua non (the essential element) of the success formula. *Determined* and *persistent* application of all the principles set forth in this book is required for the achievement of your life's goals.

By determination we mean an absolute refusal to quit. Persistence is basically the constant and consistent refusal to quit. In other words, persistence is consistently applied determination. You exhibit persistence when you never give up. Persistence is that something extra that all great achievers have.

One obvious example occurs in the boxing ring. Very often, two evenly matched fighters box round after round without either one taking a decisive lead on the judges' cards. The match is "too close to call." Basically, they are neutralizing each other's skills, and the outcome depends on which lion is hungrier, which fighter wants it so bad he can taste it, which one exhibits an absolute refusal to quit. As the match progresses into the later rounds, you can often see and feel the mind of one boxer begin to dominate. The fighter with the greater determination will invariably be victorious. There are a great many upset victories in boxing because it is almost impossible to predict an athlete's determination.

In February of 1990, journeyman boxer James "Buster" Douglas was such an underdog to "Iron" Mike Tyson that oddsmakers weren't taking bets. What chance did this "average" fighter have against the undefeated, undisputed heavyweight champion? Few people expected the fight to go more than a couple rounds. However, what they couldn't predict was Douglas's determination, fueled by the recent passing of his mother. The first devastating blow of the fight was thrown by Tyson and landed directly on Douglas's jaw. No one thought Douglas could survive this blow since no one had ever come back from a Tyson knockdown. Not only did Douglas come back, but in the next round he knocked Tyson out.

## The Importance of Consistency

The methodology of success must be used so consistently that it becomes second nature. This is why determination and persistence are so essential. Intermittent use is not sufficient to form the productive habits necessary for success. Inconsistent thoughts and actions confuse your subconscious mind by sending it contradictory signals that may ultimately cause you to veer from your chosen path.

Even after you have formed productive habits, you must always work at maintaining them. Once you begin to deviate from them, you risk sliding all the way back to where you started from—or worse.

The most prevalent example of this is weight loss. Americans always seem to be battling this bogeyman.

One can lose weight rather quickly. However, keeping it off is a major problem. All studies of weight loss indicate that the majority of people who lose weight do not exercise the determination and persistence required to maintain the desired weight. This common foible is what makes the weight-loss industry so lucrative.

Another example of the need for persistence is found in exercising. In order to achieve and maintain a healthy, fit body, you must do aerobic exercises a minimum of three days per week for at least twenty minutes each time. Fitness cannot be stored.

If you train for years and even reach the level of a decathlon champion, it will still do you no permanent good if you stop. Within a matter of weeks, you will lose most of your fitness. We have seen many people devise elaborate and extensive exercise routines. They maintain a rigid schedule and work out hours a day. This is great while it lasts. Eventually, however, they abandon their vigorous routine and lose their fitness in the process.

Many athletes (and nonathletes) develop and maintain excellent bodies by doing only a few exercises consistently. You can develop a powerful upper body by merely doing two simple exercises—push-ups and sit-backs. A person who does push-ups and sit-backs consistently will have a much better physique than someone who does extensive weight training but then stops after a few years.

Your mind works in a similar way. Luckily, the efforts of mental training are much more enduring. But the principle is the same. If you begin using the techniques set forth in this book on a regular basis, but then stop, you'll soon forget many of the lessons of success. You will fall back into old patterns of thinking and lose the edge that makes for success.

Of course, no one is consistent 100 percent of the time. However, this fact is not an excuse for not *trying* to bat a thousand. The more you strive for consistency in your daily life, the closer you will get. Gradually, the pieces will fall into place, and new patterns of thought and action will replace the old patterns of fear and inaction. After a while, your habits will become so completely ingrained that you will be totally incapable of quitting. When it comes to being a quitter, we encourage you to become a total failure.

## Practice Makes Permanent, Not Perfect

In developing determination and persistence, however, be careful that you persist on the right path. All the persistence in the world will not get you to your destination if you're driving on the wrong road. For example, the cry is often heard these days that longer school days is the key to solving the illiteracy problem and the current public education crisis in the U.S. This "solution," however, fails to recognize that many public schools are on the wrong path. If they do not teach effectively in seven hours, why do we think they will do better in ten? A piano student who isn't taught the right notes to begin with will not improve by more practice.

Constant but ineffective practicing will lead to an ingrained ineffectiveness that will be difficult to eradicate. At such times, practice does *not* make perfect. Bob Unger learned this lesson the hard way. Before discovering Jim Lynn, he had studied briefly with another voice teacher who prescribed strain-inducing vocal exercises that Bob indeed practiced zealously day after day. The more Bob vocalized, the more his vocal cords were damaged. They became so bad that Bob was forced to seek medical treatment and to remain almost totally silent for an extended period of time.

As you can see, in this situation practice certainly did not make perfect. In fact, had Bob continued with this improper technique he would have sustained permanent damage. Make sure, then, that the actions and thoughts you persistently repeat are worthy of repetition.

## Overcoming the Obstacles

Obstacles to success lie all around us, like minefields in a war zone. Discrimination, ignorance, corruption, the old-boy network, the insiders-against-the-outsiders syndrome, nepotism, family poverty, and a predominantly negative thinking environment all conspire to limit or prevent our success. Obstacles are a fact of life; they can be overcome only by persistence and determination. Whether it's Jackie Robinson breaking the color barrier in professional baseball or John F. Kennedy becoming the first Catholic president of the United States, roadblocks can be overcome. The examples are infinite: a black man by the name of General Colin Powell became Chairman of the Joint Chiefs of Staff; Sandra Day O'Connor became the first female United States Supreme Court Justice.

Unfortunately, obstacles are too often used as crutches or alibis to excuse giving up or, even worse, to excuse failure to start trying. Politicians and leaders who encourage these alibis under the guise of justice and equality do a tremendous disservice to the people victimized by this sort of exploitation. For every obstacle in the world, one can find countless numbers of people overcoming it. Achievers simply dwell on the *overcoming,* whereas nonachievers (and their manipulative exploiters) dwell on the *obstacles.*

## Getting Back into the Arena

It's natural to sometimes want to quit when you are discouraged. It's very easy to quit. Anybody can do it.

205

It takes absolutely no effort. That is why people who have determination and persistence often appear almost superhuman to the quitters.

One fine example of getting off the canvas of defeat was demonstrated by our friend and client, New York State Assemblyman Douglas Prescott. Doug has always lived and breathed politics. He wanted very badly to get into politics and began his career as staff assistant to former New York State Senator James Buckley. Doug did everything for the senator, including (but not limited to) taking constituents' complaints or driving the senator to the airport.

Several years later, in 1980, Doug Prescott was elected to the New York State Assembly out of Queens County. Doug was elated because he was doing something he loved to do and trying to make a difference doing it.

However, his biggest test was yet to come. In the 1982 election, Doug was defeated by a campaign full of lies and deceptions that newspapers characterized as the dirtiest election campaign in Queens history. Doug's opponents, just before the election, sent a mass mailing to all voters in the district. The mailing, according to local news reports, contained all sorts of deceptions and distortions designed to get voters angry at Prescott on the eve of election day. Coming at the last minute, as the mailing did, Doug had no opportunity to respond. Before he knew what had hit him, he had been unseated. To Doug, this defeat must have been devastating. Yet we remember him standing in his election headquarters all night, smiling, thanking all the workers who had stood by him, and maintaining an unshakable spirit.

The next day we found out what Doug was really made of. He demonstrated that "when the going gets tough, the tough get going." He spent all day preparing campaign literature designed to expose the alleged "dirty tricks" campaign of the new assemblyman who had defeated him. Many might ask at this point what in the world Doug was doing preparing campaign literature when the campaign was already over. The answer is that although the battle may have ended in Doug's defeat, the war was far from over.

Many people in Doug's position would have simply used their political connections to get a lucrative job, but not Doug. He wanted to be an assemblyman and he was ready, willing, and able to make whatever sacrifices were necessary to attain that goal. His wife Judy went back to work while Doug spent the next two years going door to door and speaking personally to every voter in the district; he traveled on foot to ten thousand households. As a result of this great determination, persistence, and effort, Doug regained his seat in the 1984 elections. He has won two subsequent elections by landslides. His story serves as a model to all those who refuse to lie down and play dead.

## Persistence and Determination Defuse Disadvantages

Persistence is really an attitude. However, it is so vital that we are devoting this chapter to it. We have had many successful clients who seem to lack talent, creative ability, and education. The one thing they do have, however, is persistence, and that alone is enough to create success. You can see the principle of persistence working every day. In chapter four we spoke of those Asian immigrants who come to this country not knowing the language. In fact, their native tongue bears practically no resemblance to English. Many have little or no education. Yet they do very well in this country. Why? One reason is that they are willing to work hard for long hours. Notice who runs many of the fruit stands, candy stores, laundromats, and dry cleaning establishments. Notice how many hours a day they stay open and how few vacations they take.

It is our belief that anyone, regardless of their background, can make it in the U.S.A.—and make it big. The reason is clear; no place on earth provides the opportunity that this country does. Unfortunately, most people are not sufficiently motivated to apply themselves with the requisite determination and persistence. Those who do, have unlimited potential.

As we have said, the rules for success are quite simple and easy to follow. However, most fail to use them or, if they do, they stop using them after a short time. Consequently, they get no results and deceive themselves into believing they really tried. Most people will not really try; others will put forth effort for only a time. Those few who keep trying and never give up will achieve success.

History is the story of those who persisted: Thomas Edison, Madame Curie, Abraham Lincoln, Alexander the Great, Marconi, Robert Fulton, Florence Nightingale, Helen Keller. The list is endless. As Zig Ziglar says, success in life is like pumping a well. The more you have to pump, the deeper the well and therefore the cleaner, clearer, cooler, and sweeter the water. But you never know how much more pumping you'll have to do before you hit the jackpot. One thing is certain; if you stop pumping, you will not get the water. If you refuse to stop, eventually you will be rewarded. Keep pressing on.

What is it that made these great people of history persist? Why were they able to resist the temptation to quit? When you boil it down, persistence is a function of two key ingredients, burning desire and faith.

## Burning Desire Fuels Persistence

You have to want something obsessively in order to overcome the adversity that you will certainly face. The principle of desire is well illustrated in the field of entertainment. You will notice that it is not the most talented who succeed but those who have the greatest desire. As one great entertainer once said, forget talent; it's tenacity that counts. We have had theatrical agents tell us that singers are a dime a dozen (of course, this doesn't apply to singing lawyers).

Barry Manilow is a familiar name in the music industry. He presently reaps the rewards generated by his numerous hit records. This was not always the case. The theme of Barry Manilow's recent New York tour is autobiographical; it recounts his struggle to follow his dreams, despite the odds. Manilow depicts a scene which was repeated over and over again. Manilow is the piano player accompanying young hopefuls at open auditions. Each performer is given but a few minutes to make an impression upon the director. Talent is plentiful, but talent is not the ingredient that left an indelible impression upon Barry Manilow. No. Instead, he recounts his amazement at the persistence of these performers, and his increasing respect for their spirit— that force which never allowed them to give up their personal quests, no matter how many times they were passed over.

Barry Manilow claims he learned far more from those who failed to get the part than from those who did. The tremendous desire and courage required to keep trying in the face of almost certain rejection left him in awe of these "stars." It also provided the motivation he initially lacked to pursue his own dreams. He subsequently invested his meager life savings in a band and took the show on the road. Poor planning resulted in the band

209

going bust on the West Coast. The lean years that ensued were a firsthand lesson in the art of living eco-
nomically, but he didn't give up; he never lost sight of
his dream. Odd jobs sustained him, and Manilow
worked on his original compositions whenever possible. Finally, his song "Mandy" became a hit, the first of
many, and a new star was born. Barry Manilow has said
that he paid his dues, and so he has. Yet his elation at fulfilling his dream is so great that he encourages his audience to pursue their dreams no matter what the costs
and no matter how many auditions it takes.

Barry Manilow, Frank Sinatra, Joan Rivers, Paul
Anka, and hundreds of other big-name stars did not
make it solely on the basis of their ability. There are
many talented people out there. All the stars had the
door not merely shut but slammed in their face time
and time again. But they followed an inner voice, a
strong desire. In one way or another, they were all told,
"You stink," "You have no talent," "You'll never make
it." They faced this rejection regularly. How many
people are willing to endure that kind of abuse? Not
many. Those who make it in show business all have a
strong desire. They want it so bad, they can taste it.
Without desire, there is no way they can withstand the
constant rejection and adversity. They are all driven to
succeed.

While burning desire is the first ingredient to success, the second ingredient that produces a potent persistence is faith.

## Faith Fuels Persistence

Faith is the second and most important principle in
the one-two punch that leads to persistence. Faith is
our bridge to the future. With it, you can accomplish
anything, but without it, you are permanently stuck

210

where you are. "If ye have faith ... nothing shall be impossible unto you" (Matthew 17:20).

A simple illustration will show you why faith is so necessary to persistence. Take a person drilling for oil. Obviously he must have a strong desire to find the oil; that's a given. But what if he is not even sure that there is any oil at that particular location? For how long would he drill? Now take the same person but let him see a picture of the oil underneath the rocks. We know that this person will not stop drilling until he strikes oil. Why? Because he believes the oil is there.

Faith is knowing that something is there just as strongly as if you actually see it—even if you can't see it. Faith is the mental leap that enables you to achieve your desires. True greatness is reserved for those who can develop faith. You may be advised that this is too difficult. Yet our everyday life is based on faith.

We have faith that the sun will rise in the sky. We have faith that the light will go on or off when we flick the switch. We have faith that the food we buy is not harmful to us. We have faith that our car will start. We have faith that when the light is green, we can proceed, since it must be red to the opposite traffic and drivers will stop on the red signal. These assumptions allow us to go about our daily tasks because we are able to depend on them. We have faith. But take away our faith in these things that we depend on and there will be disruption in our lives. We will find it difficult to do the necessary things. Faith makes it possible for us to concentrate on doing the necessary things.

More importantly, faith is the key that unlocks that awesome potential of our subconscious mind. The subconscious mind does whatever the conscious mind commands. It does not distinguish between good or bad, right or wrong, truth or falsehood. The subconscious accepts as true whatever *beliefs* are fed into it by the

211

conscious mind. Faith acts upon the subconscious much the way a teacher acts upon a student. The clearer and more convincing the teacher, the better the result. Likewise, the greater the faith, the clearer the transmission to the subconscious mind.

If you develop unshakable faith that something will happen, your subconscious mind works overtime to create the reality. However, if your faith wavers, then the subconscious gets confused; it is not sure whether or not to create the reality. That is one of the reasons persistence in thought is necessary to success. The more persistent your thoughts, the greater your belief becomes. With strong belief, you will be able to create the object of your desire. As William James once said, "Our belief at the beginning of a doubtful undertaking is the one thing that ensures the successful outcome of the venture."

The process also works in reverse. If you lack faith, your subconscious mind will work just as hard to reward your lack of faith. It will ensure that you do not achieve that which you believe you cannot do. If you say you can do it, you probably will. If you say you cannot do it, you probably won't. As always, the choice is yours.

This is why negative thoughts are so deadly. They carry with them the same self-fulfilling potential as do positive thoughts. Again, your subconscious mind will work either way. If you're positive, it will work to achieve the positive. If you're negative, it will work to achieve the negative. That is why history is about those who have had faith. Those who lacked faith never achieved, because they had no faith that they could achieve.

Faith, like anything else, can be developed. This is one of the great secrets of success. Many people think that faith is something you either have or you haven't. This is not so. Faith can be developed. How? By using

212

the techniques described in this book. As we stated in chapter five, the two key techniques are: 1) self-talk (or affirmations) and 2) visualization. These methods instruct the mind to believe.

By visualizing what you want to occur, you start believing it is possible. Your mind starts working to complete in reality the pictures you have in your mind. Self-talk essentially saturates your mind with orders. By constant repetition of these orders—that the future event will in fact occur—your faith grows.

However, if you are inconsistent with your visualization and self-talk, injecting occasional doubt, then faith will weaken. With weak faith comes weak results. That is why you should avoid negative self-talk at all times. More importantly, you should avoid verbalizing negative thoughts. These statements, even when said in jest, carry powerful repercussions. They confuse your subconscious mind. You'll notice that extremely determined individuals rarely joke about their important ambitions. They stay determined by refusing to let in any negative thoughts, no matter how innocuous they may seem.

So desire and faith, acting together, practically guarantee persistent effort. If you lack desire or faith, you cannot mount a persistent effort.

Now that we have covered the two master keys to determination and persistence, we can offer three additional ways to shore up your ability to keep your chin up: shrugging off setbacks, maintaining patience, and developing the finishing habit.

## Shrugging Off Setbacks

Refuse to worry about your failures and mistakes. People who fear these things will never be able to let it all hang out. All top performers are able to do just that.

213

They push themselves out of the comfort zone and into that field where only the great consistently play. Anyone who goes all out and puts himself on the line day in and day out will inevitably make mistakes.

A classic case occurred with the Coca-Cola Corporation. Beginning to lose market share to competing Pepsi-Cola, they decided to change their formula and come up with a new taste for Coke. The result was a total disaster; the public decided it preferred the old formula. Instead of despairing, Coca-Cola executives proved that they were "the real thing." They capitalized on this "setback" by marketing the abandoned formula as Classic Coke. At the same time, they continued to sell the new formula, thus effectively increasing their total market share.

Perhaps shrugging off setbacks is best exemplified by the story of a man who kept trying and trying and trying. In 1831, he failed in business. In 1832, he ran for the state legislature and lost. In 1833, he was again unable to succeed in business. The woman he loved died in 1835. In 1836, he suffered from severe depression. In 1843, he was unable to gain support in his bid for a congressional seat. In 1855, he ran for the Senate and lost. In 1856, he was considered as a vice-presidential candidate but met the same result. In 1858, he ran for the Senate and lost again. In 1860, he was elected president of the United States. Abraham Lincoln must have known about the mental-music technique. He probably kept singing that old song, "Pick yourself up, dust yourself off, and start all over again."

Do not allow yourself to dwell on mistakes. Dwelling on mistakes will cause you to make more of them. As you think, you will create circumstances consistent with your thoughts. Shake off your mistakes and enthusiastically take another whack at it.

## Learning Patience

A failure to exercise patience will cause you to become easily discouraged. Be happy for the small steps as well as the giant steps on your way to your goal. If your goal could be achieved so quickly that patience was unnecessary, the goal would probably not be worth waiting for. Remember, you have not failed unless you think you have. You have not failed unless you allow yourself to quit. You have not failed unless you turn a temporary setback into a permanent defeat by quitting. As we said in chapter three, turning your setbacks into victories by learning from them is the mark of a true winner.

The patience of a saint was required by Anne Sullivan when she came to the home of young Helen Keller. As a toddler, Helen had developed a fever that left her totally blind and deaf. Being trapped in the darkness made the little girl angry and frustrated. Anne persisted with patience, determination, and above all, love. Each day, Anne would use her fingers to "shape" letters and words inside Helen's hand. But she could not make Helen understand that this shaping had purpose. Young Helen simply thought it was a fun game. Anyone but Anne would have given up. Only her awe-inspiring faith and patience kept her going. She held tight to her indefatigable belief that Helen would eventually be able to communicate. One day, seemingly by chance, Anne ran water over Helen's palm. Helen's face lit up with joy as Anne shaped "water" upon Helen's hand. She understood! From that point on, Helen soaked up words and knowledge insatiably. She devoted the rest of her life to opening the eyes of the blind and sighted public alike. And it all started with the patience of a dedicated teacher.

## The Habit of Finishing

Determination is a habitual pattern. So is quitting. We have all known people who are great starters. Like the proverbial hare, they start off quick, raring to go, but somewhere down the road they fade into the sunset, just like the hare. But we have also known individuals who bear the tortoise's attributes of determination and persistence. They may even lack the natural physical attributes and talents of the hare, but, like "Ol' Man River," they "just keep rolling along."

Get into the habit of finishing whatever you start, even the most mundane chores. Though the chore itself may be of little consequence, forming a consistent habit of seeing every endeavor through to its conclusion will pay off for you in the long run. On the other hand, quitting even the most menial task will have a debilitating effect, making it more natural for you to quit during an important job.

We have intentionally saved this chapter for the last. We decided to do this because determination and persistence result from the consistent use of the principles outlined in all of the previous chapters. For example, when you realize that *you are responsible,* you will continue to persist, because you realize that you can exercise control over your life. People who give up feel that they are governed by factors beyond their control. People who give up constantly refer to a lack of luck or breaks. The fact is that the more persistent you are, the "luckier" you become.

Goals provide us with a reason to persist: *You'll get there if you know where you're going.* A worthy goal creates a vision which excites and generates motivation that cannot be deterred by "bad breaks."

Planning provides us with a road to travel on. Each incremental accomplishment leads us from road to highway to superhighway.

A healthy *attitude* enables us to increasingly raise our *altitude*. It provides a mental state to fuel our trip to the top. Proper attitude will create those favorable circumstances or breaks. Attitude will sustain you as you *work* toward those breaks.

Channeling your sexual energy gives you the incentive to discipline yourself and harness your instinctual drives in order to effectively use the tremendous energies these drives supply. Effective sexual channeling prevents you from taking dangerous detours.

With determination and persistence, work at incorporating these ideas into your daily life. Determination and persistence beget positive results, which beget determination and persistence.

## You Are Not Average

Without determination and persistence, no idea—regardless of its inherent value—will be brought to fruition. The next time someone tells you that "only one out of ten thousand" people can succeed, remember this. Statistics, by definition, are based on averages. Therefore, they can only be applied to the "average person." Who is this "average person" anyway? Does this person exist, or is this some fictitious concept concocted by the "experts"?

You are *not* average. Like a fingerprint, you cannot be duplicated or replaced with someone exactly like you. You are unique.

You were born to be a winner. Claim your birthright. Accept the responsibility God has given you. Set goals. Develop and execute your plan of attainment. Carry it through with a positive mental attitude. Channel your energies and throw yourself headfirst into your chosen quest, and never, never, never give up!

217

# EPILOGUE

Congratulations! You are a winner. You are on your way to greater achievement. By purchasing this book, you have shown a desire to keep improving. Wonderful things will happen to you and for you as long as you keep thinking and acting upon this desire.

Yes, you are a winner. Whether you have a net worth of seven figures or no figures is immaterial. Where you are now has absolutely nothing to do with where you can be. Keep thinking of the countless number of people who started no better off than you are right now. If they could do it, what makes you so different? Nothing, of course!

You were made in God's image, but you are *you*. You are not the economic, ethnic, or religious group you belong to—you are the only one of you there is! Make that one person matter! Make a difference in that life! Rejoice in your uniqueness and individuality. Strike out on your own path, and don't worry about whether others have walked it before you.

Remember also that reading one book does not create a successful life. You must continue feeding your mind that positive software we spoke about. Be ever vigilant and on guard against the weeds that grow in an untended mind. Read! Listen! Implant new potential!

Finally, we call upon you to help unify Americans around the principles that laid the foundation for this blessed country. We must strive to rekindle and reinstitutionalize the patriotic values that have been all too often subverted by the "blame America first" crowd. Better selves make a better life. Strengthened lives make a strong nation, and in turn that strength will flow back again and again.

It is time for a rebirth in America and in all of us. Our deepest hope is that this book will help to plant a few more seeds. It is up to each of us to nurture those seeds. We can all be part of America's new beginning.

We are happy to help any one of you as long as you are willing to help yourself. You can reach us at 516-829-3508 to schedule a seminar or just to talk.

If this book has enhanced your life in any way, all we ask in return is that you do the same for others who are looking for a hand up instead of a handout.

If you would like further information about the authors' seminars or about the book, write to:

Kupillas, Unger & Kupillas Law Offices
316 Great Neck Road
Great Neck, NY 11021